I0815832

Knitting Cowlettes

CLEVER TECHNIQUES FOR MAKING CUSTOM MINI-COWLS TO ELEVATE ANY OUTFIT

Safiyyah Talley

Storey Publishing

The mission of Storey Publishing is to serve our customers by publishing practical information that encourages personal independence in harmony with the environment.

EDITED BY Emily Spiegelman
TECH EDIT BY Kristina McGrath and Sarah Walworth
ART DIRECTION AND BOOK DESIGN BY Bredna Lago
TEXT PRODUCTION BY Jennifer Jepson Smith

COVER PHOTOGRAPHY BY © Jasminefaithphotography, front, back (author); Mars Vilaubi © Storey Publishing, spine, back (all but author)
INTERIOR PHOTOGRAPHY BY Mars Vilaubi © Storey Publishing
INTERIOR MAKEUP STYLING BY Sonya Heimann
ILLUSTRATIONS BY Alison Kolesar

Storey Publishing
210 MASS MoCA Way
North Adams, MA 01247
storey.com

Storey Publishing is an imprint of Workman Publishing, a division of Hachette Book Group, Inc., 1290 Avenue of the Americas, New York, NY 10104. The Storey Publishing name and logo are registered trademarks of Hachette Book Group, Inc.

ISBNs: 978-1-63586-801-2 (hardcover); 978-1-63586-821-0 (ebook)

Printed in China by Toppan Leefung Printing Ltd. on paper from responsible sources
10 9 8 7 6 5 4 3 2 1

TLF

Library of Congress Cataloging-in-Publication Data on file

To my loving husband, Jake, and my son, Beau

CONTENTS

Chapter 3: The Cowlette Patterns 41

Foreword

Safiyyah Talley first came into my life—virtually—back in 2020. We were months into Covid; all travel and work had stopped. I remember joking to a friend on Zoom that there was nothing to do but drink wine and knit, and I might as well call myself "the drunk knitter." She answered, "You can't. There already is one!" I ran to check out @drunkknitter on Instagram. There she was, a huge grin on her face, balancing two cakes of yarn on her head. That's Safiyyah—she can find fun even in the middle of a world-wide pandemic.

I quickly became a regular visitor. Her account had everything I needed: a cat, a dog, an adorable baby, and knitting. Lots and lots of knitting. The next year, she combined her passion for knitting and her playful spirit in one of the most epic internet gags that I've ever seen. She shamelessly knit her husband's Christmas present right in front of him to see if he'd notice. Spoiler alert: He didn't.

That spirit of adventure, playfulness, and fun permeates every aspect of Safiyyah's work. She and I worked together at a knitting retreat shortly after the publication of her brilliant book *Knit 2 Socks in 1*. We were chatting about her new book, and when I asked her why socks, she said, "Because they're FUUUUUN."

This, in a nutshell, is Safiyyah's approach to knitting. She has an amazing ability to make knitting simple, approachable, and just plain fun.

Now she's done it again with *Knitting Cowlettes*. With the words "All you need to get started is a ball of yarn, circular knitting needles, and a sense of adventure," Safiyyah has created a knitting party where all are welcome.

There is no "right" way to do things here. You can be a planner or a wing-it knitter. There's no judgment in this book, just an honest assessment of the options. The "design every step of the way" approach may take more planning, the "grab your needles and go" approach may take a bit of ripping. Both roads lead to happiness.

But most important, this book is filled with the space and encouragement to play. You can experiment with cables, lace, colorwork, marling, simple texture stitches (the Goldenrod and Twill patterns are particular faves of mine)—anything. Cowlettes are fast and small, so go wild!

As Safiyyah so encouragingly reminds us, every cowlette starts with just three stitches. So, grab a ball of yarn and needles and join the party. I promise, you'll be glad you came.

Patty Lyons

Why Cowlettes?

When I first started seriously knitting, meaning, when a day didn't go by without my picking up my needles, I became obsessed with making gifts. I loved creating something that would be cherished by the recipient. That said, I am also a procrastinator, so I would often wait until the very last minute to get started. A day or two before a birthday I would make the 45-minute drive to my local yarn shop to buy yarn (in Midwest terms, this is a quick drive!), head straight home, and immediately cast on. Once my yarn and needles were ready to go, I would turn to my favorite gift-giving project: a cowlette.

I like to gift cowlettes because they are quick, gender neutral, size inclusive, and very useful. There are just so many scenarios that call for one that I even gift them to myself. Wake up to a chill in the air? Pop on a cowlette. Want to dress up an outfit? Pop on a cowlette. Need to show off a knitted item at the knitting convention, and it's a very hot and crowded July day? Say it with me now: "Pop on a cowlette!"

You might be wondering, "What exactly is a cowlette?" *Cowlette* is a term created by innovative knitwear designer Carina Spencer and it is the lovechild of a cowl—a circular scarf—and a shawlette, or a small shawl. Cowlettes have a similar construction to a shawl, but with the wearability of a cowl. Shawls tend to slip and slide when worn, unless secured in some way with a knot or a shawl pin. Cowlettes look like shawls, but they are knit in the round, so the wearer doesn't have to worry about them falling off. Just like shawls, cowlettes are first worked flat from the top down. Stitches are added in the form of increases until the work is large enough to fit comfortably around the wearer's neck. The cowlette is then joined in the round and worked to the desired size and length. When searching online for cowlette patterns, you may find them under "cowls" or "shawls," because it is a fairly new knitting term.

In addition to being the perfect last-minute gift, cowlettes are my go-to accessory because they elevate any outfit. Whether paired with dresses, jeans, leggings, or anything in between, a handmade cowlette makes any outfit better. It adds warmth when knit in a bulky wool and draped over a winter coat. Alternatively, a DK or worsted weight cotton cowlette is the perfect companion to keep the chill off on cool summer nights. When knit in an airy mohair or silk lace, a cowlette lends a touch of sophistication that can be effortlessly layered over formal attire.

But the very best part of making cowlettes is how customizable they are. With the help of this book, you can easily design your own. You can control the difficulty, size, yarn amount, and gauge with very little prep and only as much math as you wish! It is the perfect project for all knitters, from beginner to expert. All you need to get started is a ball of yarn, circular knitting needles, and a sense of adventure.

How to Use This Book

This book is designed as a guide to help you create your dream cowlette, with or without a pattern. So where to start? I recommend reading Chapters 1 and 2 first, to ensure that you have all the necessary information to successfully embark on your cowlette knitting journey. Then I invite you to cast on either The Triangle (page 42) or The Half-Pi (page 45). After completing your first cowlette, you can then choose from two paths: Follow one of the other patterns in Chapter 3, or, if you are feeling extra adventurous, use the techniques taught in Chapter 2 and the Cowlette Knitter's Worksheet (page 112) to design your own. Whichever path you choose, know that this is YOUR adventure. Stay within familiar comforts or take your knitting to the far corners of your imagination. Choose the option that brings you the most joy and fulfillment.

CHAPTER 1

Choose Your Story

Your adventure begins here. Think of this chapter as your home base. It covers some basics that will help you choose your yarn, needles, and gauge, as well as other supplies that will prepare you to embark on your cowlette knitting journey.

If you enjoy a little unpredictability, like I do, then you can knit a cowlette with minimal planning and nothing more than a ball of yarn and appropriately sized needles. Of course, results will vary, and that can be part of the fun. However, if you wish for more control over your outcome, then you need to understand how your yarn, needles, and notions will affect your finished cowlette. In this chapter I guide you through some of the tools of the cowlette trade.

Choosing the Right Yarn for Your Cowlette

Yarn is the building block of a knitting project. Understanding how your yarn choice interacts with a pattern or design is so important. Many of my students are surprised at how different yarns can drastically affect the look and feel of a finished design. One of my favorite party tricks as a knitting instructor is to show two sweaters knit from the same pattern, one made with merino and the other with acrylic. The difference between the two garments in terms of their drape, fit, and function is so stark, it's shocking. The merino sweater has a soft drape that flows with the body, while the acrylic version is thick, almost unforgiving, and looks as if it can stand up on its own. Of course, there is a time and a place for knitting with both fibers. In this section I will explain how to make the best choice for your needs.

In the patterns in Chapter 3, I chose an array of fibers to achieve a variety of different looks. Want a cowlette that can outlast the toughest weather conditions? Pure, untreated, raw wool will be your top choice. Need a cowlette that will delicately drape over the bride's shoulders at the ceremony? Say hello to my friends mohair and silk.

There are so many fiber options and blends to choose from that you may find yourself with more than a handful of favorites. I like to branch out every now and then and experiment with different types of fiber. Within the yarn industry, there are three main fiber types: animal, plant-based, and synthetic.

Animal Fibers

Fiber artists have used materials as common as wool, alpaca, and silk and as unusual as human and dog hair. The link between all these fibers is that they are made of animal proteins, sourced from hair or fur or made by insects. These proteins wick moisture, resulting in yarn that is warm in the winter and cool in the summer. Thus, yarns made of animal fibers create versatile garments that can be worn year-round.

WOOL. Almost all of the cowlettes in this book contain wool. Wool is my favorite fiber for cowlettes because it is just so forgiving. It keeps its shape through countless wears, making it a predictable fiber to work with, unlike alpaca, which has a tendency to grow with wear. Its ability to be easily blocked allows you to manipulate lace, cable, or textured stitches after binding off. If a wool cowlette is a smidge too small, or maybe the center point isn't, well, pointy enough, all you need to do is wash it and pin it into shape (see page 19).

Wool's warmth and ability to hold its shape make it an ideal fiber for cowlettes.
Cool and airy, cotton is perfect for summer-weight knits.

Plant-Based Fibers

Derived from cellulose (the main component in plant cell walls), fibers can be sourced from plants such as bamboo, seaweed, flax, and cotton. Yarn made from plant-based fibers absorbs moisture and becomes stronger when wet. These qualities make cotton yarn a great choice for washcloths. Yarns made from plant-based fibers also have incredible breathability. Because they draw heat away from the body, they are ideal for summer garments. Plant-based fibers are also perfect for those who wish to avoid animal by-products. Although plant-based fibers lack the elasticity of protein-packed animal fibers, they still offer a beautiful drape. After washing, your lacework will literally bloom. Your cables may not be plump and three dimensional if knit in 100 percent plant-based yarn, but they will be drapey and lacey. The spaces between the stitches will open and expose the gap between the cable twist and the background stitches, creating an airy, ethereal fabric.

COTTON. Cotton cowlettes are a fan favorite in the warmer months. They breathe well, are resilient to wear, and are gentle enough for babies and children with sensitive skin. When knitting cowlettes with cotton, remember that cotton tends to grow and lose its shape with wear. It's important to accommodate for cotton's "slouch," or simply embrace the slouch as a relaxed design element. I also like to utilize cotton's airiness by using it to knit lace.

Synthetic Fibers

Designed to improve on natural animal and plant fibers, synthetic fibers are produced in a laboratory. Yarns made with synthetic fibers have long been beloved by knitters sensitive to animal fibers. Popular synthetic fibers include acrylic, nylon, and polyester. Unfortunately, synthetic fibers are not always environmentally friendly. The most popular is acrylic, which is made from petroleum and is essentially plastic that has been stretched and spun into a fiber. And so, like plastic, acrylic fiber is durable, but it is also heat sensitive (though less so now than it used to be) and lacks breathability. Yarns made from these fibers create strong, long-lasting garments that are easy to care for, and they can be more affordable than wool, but they do not breathe or wick moisture well.

ACRYLIC. Acrylic is a good option for those who prefer not to wear or knit with animal fibers but want to make a warm cowlette. Rather than using 100 percent acrylic yarn, I prefer a blend with wool or cotton. These blended yarns showcase the better qualities of each fiber. For example, the wool adds wicking properties and warmth, while the acrylic provides easy laundry care.

USING ACRYLIC YARNS RESPONSIBLY

I often joke that projects made from acrylic yarn will outlive us, but really, there is truth to that statement. My mom has an afghan that my grandmother crocheted out of acrylic scraps in the 1970s. My mom machine washes and dries it, then drapes it on the back of her couch where it is leaned against, snuggled with, and kneaded by cat claws until the next laundry day. Despite the abuse, this 60-year-old blanket still has a lot of life, and not a single hole!

According to my friends at Darn Good Yarn, an online retailer of sustainably sourced yarn, it can take up to 200 years for acrylic yarn to break down (hence this 60-year-old blanket still going strong!). But when it does, it leaches microplastic into our waterways. So why do I champion synthetic yarns? In addition to synthetic fibers' durability and warmth, the advancements that have been made in the synthetic fiber industry are amazing. You can walk into any big box store and buy a giant skein of synthetic yarn for $5 that was created responsibly with 100 percent recycled materials.

My advice when buying synthetic yarn is to buy only what you need for the intended project. Avoid throwing away any unused yarn so it doesn't end up in a landfill. Once your project is complete, cherish it or give it to someone else who will love it, too. And maybe your project will also join the sexagenarian club, like my grandmother's afghan.

Yarn Weight

Yarn companies classify their yarns by weight, which represents the thickness of the strand of yarn. Industry standard yarn weights are lace, fingering, sport, DK, worsted, bulky, and super bulky. Below, I list the most common weights for cowlette knitting.

Lace

The thinnest weight of yarn produces an extremely fine fabric that is deliciously light and airy. Wearing a cowlette knit from a lace weight yarn is almost like wearing a cloud around your neck. It won't necessarily add a lot of warmth, but it will be a comfortable, fashionable layer that creates interest and adds texture to your outfit.

True confession: I hardly ever knit other projects with a lace weight yarn. As a person who thrives off instant gratification, I tend to reach for thicker yarns. However, because cowlettes are so easy and quick, I select lace weight for my cowlettes more often, and I love that you can get up to (and sometimes even more than) 545 yards (498 meters) in a 100-gram skein.

When knitting with lace weight yarn, I like to use needles a size or two larger than what the ball band suggests in order to really capitalize on the airiness and also to speed up the knitting time. And although this weight of yarn is perfect for lace motifs, I prefer either stockinette or garter stitch, both of which create a cowlette with beautiful drape.

Fingering

Fingering weight yarn is my personal favorite for knitting cowlettes. It is slightly thicker than lace weight, so it is a little bit faster to knit with, and it's a more common weight of yarn, so it's easier to find in yarn shops and big box stores.

When picking yarn for a cowlette, my first instinct is to pull hanks of fingering weight from my stash to compare and mull over. A 100-gram skein of fingering weight yarn usually yields 370–460 yards (339–421 meters), which is more than enough yardage for a cowlette. Fingering weight yarn can also be used in so many ways. It looks great when worked with the suggested US 0 (2 mm) to 2 (2.75 mm) needle and makes for a warm and hardwearing cowlette. Or, you can go up to a US 7 (4.5 mm) needle to knit a fabric that's airy and light, to be worn on special occasions.

Sport

Sport weight yarn can also be used to create lightweight cowlettes. A sport weight yarn will knit up slightly faster than a fingering weight yarn, so it is an ideal choice for knitters who want a lightweight cowlette without the time commitment a fingering weight gauge requires. The only reason I don't use sport weight as often as fingering is simply because a lot of my favorite yarn bases just happen to be fingering. There is also slightly less yardage, 290–360 yards (265–329 meters), in a sport weight skein.

DK

Next in line is DK weight. DK weight yarn is my favorite choice for socks, cardigans, hats, and mittens because it's just thick enough to produce a quick project without compromising drape. Because I use it so frequently for large projects, I often have an odd skein or two of DK left over in my stash, which is the perfect amount of yarn for a cowlette. A DK weight cowlette will drape gorgeously and provide warmth. Lace motifs will look chunkier and lack the airiness that finer gauges provide, while still providing interest and texture. The generous 240–280 yards (220–256 meters) in a 100-gram skein will yield enough that you won't have to worry about needing more than one skein!

DK IS FOR . . .

Did you know that DK stands for double knit? Here, *double knit* refers to the yarn weight, not the knitting technique that lets you simultaneously create two layers of fabric. Want to knit a DK weight cowlette but only have fingering weight yarn on hand? Holding two strands of fingering weight will yield a DK to worsted weight! This is also a great way to stash bust and experiment with color.

Worsted and Aran

Cowlettes knit in worsted or Aran weight yarns are the way to go for beginners. Worsted weight is thicker than DK weight, and Aran weight is slightly thicker than worsted weight. Both worsted and Aran weight cowlettes will keep you warm on snowy days, and knitters can relish the heavier gauge that works up in the blink of an eye. The 170–220 yards (156–201 meters) of yarn in a 100-gram skein will be plenty for a small or medium-size cowlette.

Bulky and Super Bulky

As I have mentioned previously, I'm a glutton for an instant gratification project. And I like to be warm. When knit in bulky or super bulky yarn, cowlettes become this fuzzy, warm hug that I just cannot help but wear all day. Because thicker yarns tend to show every imperfection (you know, with the stitches being so big and all), I like to keep things simple by focusing on creating clean lines on basic fabrics. So, stockinette, slipped stitches, simple cables, and lace motifs are my favorite tricks to pull out when working with bulky and super bulky yarn. You will typically get 100–170 yards (92–156 meters) of yarn per 100-gram ball, so you will need 2–3 skeins for a larger cowlette.

HOW MUCH YARN?

Just like people, cowlettes come in a variety of shapes and sizes. The patterns in this book range in size from a kerchief to a capelet, and I even included a baby cowlette! Each one lists the yardage required, but what if you are planning on designing your own? Don't worry, I have you covered!

Smaller cowlettes only require one skein, 50 to 100 grams of yarn.

Medium-size cowlettes use 100 to 200 grams of yarn.

Large-size cowlettes require 200 to 400 grams of yarn.

When in doubt, always buy an extra skein. It's better to have some leftover yarn than to not have enough to finish your cowlette.

Choosing Needles for Your Project

Cowlettes are first worked flat, with stitches added until the work is large enough to fit comfortably around the neck. The cowlette is then worked in the round until it reaches the desired size. Working in the round is a common knitting pattern instruction. When you join a cowlette to knit in the round, instead of turning your knitting at the end of the last row, you work in a continuous spiral by immediately knitting into the first cast-on stitch. In this book, this is referred to as "joining in the round."

After knitting into each of the remaining stitches on your needle, you will start the second round by knitting into the first stitch of the first round, then continue knitting into the stitches you made in the previous round, forming a piece of circular knitting. I suggest using a stitch marker (page 22) to mark the beginning of the round. This will help you keep track of the rounds as you knit.

Use Circular Needles

The term *circular needle* is used to describe a pair of knitting needles attached by a cord. A circular needle allows you to knit continuously in the round. Even though cowlettes are knit flat before being joined and worked in the round, I use a circular needle for both steps. It's not only possible to knit flat on them, it's also quite comfortable because the needle tips are shorter than straight needles, making them more ergonomic.

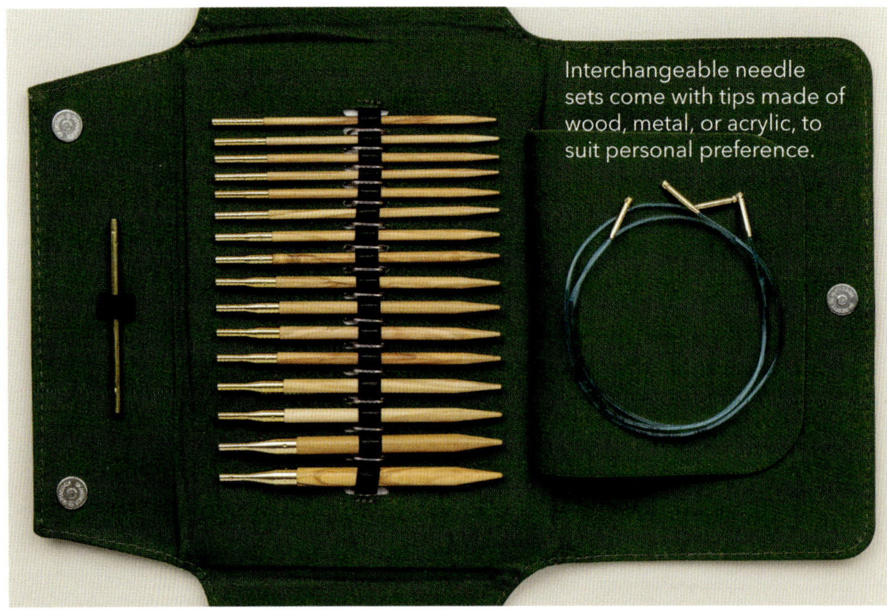

Interchangeable needle sets come with tips made of wood, metal, or acrylic, to suit personal preference.

INTERCHANGEABLE IS BEST. When knitting cowlettes I prefer to use interchangeable needles. They allow you to swap out cords of different lengths by either screwing or snapping them into place. You can begin with a shorter cord, and then gradually increase the cord length to accommodate more stitches as the project grows.

TRY BEFORE YOU BUY

Before investing in a set of interchangeable circular needles, my best advice is to visit your local yarn store to see if they have any needles to try out, or purchase one pair of needle tips and one cord for a fraction of the price of an entire set.

Another option is to ask a fellow knitter if you can try out their needle set. I am just dying for someone to ask me about my (now discontinued) circular needle set, which is the Addi Click Mixed Set. It is a "mixed set" because each pair contains one sharp needle and one standard needle. The sharper needle is perfect for working intricate stitches like lace and cables on the right side of your work. When you turn to the wrong side, which is usually made up of purl stitches, the standard, duller needle makes for speedy purling without splitting stitches.

NEEDLE LENGTH. I usually begin on a circular needle that measures 24 inches (60 cm) from needle tip to needle tip. This length allows me to join my work in the round easily. (Typically, the neck opening of a cowlette is around 20–24 inches [50–60 cm].) If a pattern requires increases or adding more stitches after joining in the round, you may have to switch to a 32-inch (80 cm) circular needle to accommodate the additional stitches.

Choosing the Right Needle Size

When knitting cowlettes, a looser gauge is beneficial because it guarantees that increases will lie flat (tightly knitted cowlettes can appear wrinkled and puckered). If you are unsure about which size needle to pair with your yarn, a great rule of thumb is to choose the largest needle size suggested on the yarn's ball band. For example, Blue Sky Fibers recommends using US 9 (5.5 mm) to US 11 (8 mm) needles for Woolstok Tweed Aran yarn, so I would suggest knitting with US 11 (8 mm) needles.

To Swatch or Not to Swatch

A swatch is a small sample of knitting, usually a 4 × 4-inch (10 × 10 cm) square made with the same yarn, needles, and stitches you are using for your project.

Usually when you make a gauge swatch, you are mostly concerned with determining stitch count because it impacts the final width of your project, which is harder to adjust later. The height is more flexible because you can simply add or take away rows to reach your desired length.

Find the Row Gauge

Swatching for cowlettes is a bit different because we are only focused on calculating one measurement: row gauge. Row gauge is the number of rows in 4 inches (10 centimeters). Once you find your row gauge, you can easily figure out how many rows you need to work to reach the desired size of the neck opening. (For a sneak peek on how to do this, turn to page 34.)

I figured this out one day when the size of a cowlette I was working on didn't match with my desired stitch count measurement. I had calculated it correctly, but it was just too small! Frustrated, I pulled the stitches off my needles and took a good look at the shape of what I was knitting. That's when I realized that my design approach had been focused on the wrong gauge. Because we are starting from the straight edge of a semicircle or the point of a triangle, we always cast on fewer stitches to start, then strategically add increases and work rows until the cowlette reaches the desired size.

So, when we swatch for cowlettes, we will be checking for our row count only.

MAKE A SWATCH. Cast on enough stitches to create at least 4 inches (10 centimeters) of knitting, plus 3 extra stitches at each end for creating edges (see page 35 for more on edge stitches). You can get an idea of how many stitches this will be by checking your yarn's ball band. Many ball bands state the number of stitches you need, along with the recommended needle size. Knit flat using the stitch pattern you plan to use for the body of the cowlette until your work measures 4 inches (10 centimeters) from the cast on.

Loosely bind off your stitches, then wash and dry the swatch according to the instructions on the yarn's ball band. Do not skip this step! For more about the importance of washing and drying your swatch, see Blocking on page 19. Lay the piece on a flat surface and measure the number of rows in 4 inches (10 centimeters) using a swatch gauge ruler. Divide the number of rows by 4 for inches or 10 for centimeters, being sure to round to the nearest half row. Record this number on the Cowlette Knitter's Worksheet on page 112.

To get an accurate row gauge, make sure you knit at least 4 inches between the top and bottom edges of your swatch.

You can, of course, simply knit until the neck opening of your cowlette is large enough to slide over your head. But when I don't swatch first, I find the neck openings are sometimes too wide, creating the dreaded bib effect, where the cowlette fits more like a baby bib (see my Li'l One pattern on page 91) instead of sitting on your neck and shoulders like a scarf. Other times, my stitches are tighter than what the ball band suggested, resulting in fabric that lacks the drape I desired and causing me to rip it out and start over. This extra work, of course, can be easily avoided by swatching. So, if you're not sure you need to swatch, just swatch. It'll take a little time, but the peace of mind and potential for less work in the long run will be worth it.

THE MULTI SWATCH

I love to add some pizzazz to the bottom edge of a cowlette. Sometimes it's a sideways edging, or a frilly lace, or even cables. Whatever design element you decide to add, I highly recommend working a few inches of your desired motifs as part of your swatch. This will tell you how different motifs interact with each other, which will help you avoid producing a fabric that puckers or is otherwise undesirably shaped. For example, cables tend to pull the fabric in and drastically affect your gauge, while lace can change the shape of the fabric altogether, widening or elongating it depending on the stitch pattern.

T pins and a blocking mat help stretch and accentuate intricate lace motifs.

Blocking

After you finish knitting your cowlette, it is time to block. Blocking is when you launder your knits, which allows the stitches to relax completely, letting you see your true stitch gauge. Blocking also gives you a better sense of how the fabric will drape and hang. Here are the three best blocking methods, along with the pros and cons of each.

SOAK AND DRY FLAT. This is the simplest, most no-nonsense way to block. Wash your cowlette per the ball band instructions, squeeze out as much water as you can, and lay it on a flat surface to dry. Although you can use a specially made blocking mat like the one shown above, a towel, ironing board, or yoga mat works, too. Stretch the fabric to the pattern's finished dimensions or the desired size, and pin.

After it dries, there may be creases, which may crinkle any lace motifs and give your project an unfinished look. To erase them, I recommend hanging your cowlette over the bar of a wooden hanger and giving it a gentle steam.

STEAMING. I have a love-hate relationship with steamers. Have you ever had a fine fingering weight yarn get caught in the grill of a boiling-hot steamer? I have. And I never forgave or forgot (the steamer, that is). Steamers are bulky, and the smaller, light-weight ones designed for travel are slow to heat and only hold a thimble's worth of water. In a pinch, I have used a whistling kettle, a pot of boiling spaghetti, and my husband's shower.

As long as the fabric gets a touch of steam, the creases will soften and iron out on their own.

To steam a cowlette, hang it gently on the bar of a clothes hanger, preferably made from wood. Hold the steamer an inch or two away from the fabric and slowly move the steamer across it. Be sure to keep moving slowly until the entire project is damp and warm. I like to go from top to bottom, and then flip the hanger and repeat on the other side. I pay extra attention to the neckline and the cast-off edge, as both tend to roll depending on the gauge. When you are done, keep it on the hanger to dry. This will help open up the stitches and the neckline. As soon as it is dry, remove it from the hanger to avoid any stretching.

The one downside of steaming is that it may keep any intricate lace or even the neckline from lying pristinely flat. Most people are perfectly fine with this. Garments warp with wear due to the heat and moisture from our bodies, so any pristine line will be crumpled slightly anyway.

IRONING. Yes, you heard me, you can straight up iron your cowlette. An iron has even more heat than a steamer, so avoid using this method on heat-sensitive synthetic fibers, which could potentially melt. Before ironing, wash your knits and dry flat. This allows the stitches to expand and relax to their true shape and size (and also prevents the heat of the iron from setting any stains).

Next, slide your cowlette around an ironing board so that you are only working a single layer of fabric at a time. We don't want to create creases, right? Grab a tea towel. (I use a white one that has been washed several times, to eliminate any chance of color transfer from the towel to the knit.) Soak it in water (any temperature is fine), wring it out, then gently lay it over the section you wish to iron first. Because of a cowlette's circular shape, it's hard to iron it in one go, so focus on small sections that can be laid flat.

Set your iron's heat to medium or medium-high. When it's warm, iron the towel and glide it smoothly across your work. At this point you want two things: to hear a scary hissing sound and see steam. If you don't, add more water to the towel or turn up the heat slightly on your iron. As you press, keep moving the iron slowly, making sure each section is getting damp and hot. Pay extra attention to the bind off and to the neckline, and avoid any ribbing as it needs to be tighter for fit and stability reasons.

I often check on my cowlette throughout this process because nine times out of ten, my iron isn't hot enough, and I admit that I am scared of scorching my work. But do not fear! As long as your towel is damp, you hear hissing, see steam, and the iron is moving, your cowlette will not only survive, it will be even more stunning than it was before.

In addition to critical information about yarn weight and yardage, ball bands provide care instructions for preserving the beauty of your handknits.

When you are done, gently drape the project over the bar of a hanger. As soon as it is dry, remove it from the hanger and store flat.

The Ball Band Knows Best

You may have noticed that I've used the phrase *ball band* quite a bit in the past couple of sections. A ball band is literally the band of paper wrapped around a skein or ball of yarn. In some countries, yarn companies are legally required to include on this label the exact composition of the fiber, yardage, and laundering instructions, among other information about the yarn and the company that manufactured it.

When blocking your swatch, it is imperative to use the yarn company's specific instructions on laundering the yarn. Please know that I am speaking from experience. I have accidentally felted many, many projects in my lifetime!

Also, be aware that just because a yarn contains superwash wool, it doesn't necessarily mean you can put the finished garment in a washer and/or dryer. Some yarns contain a blend of superwash wool and other fibers that must be hand laundered. To be safe, always remember that the ball band knows best.

Notions

Notions are the additional tools that a knitter needs to complete a project. This list covers the notions you'll commonly need when knitting a cowlette.

MEASURING TAPE. This will be your best friend because it allows you to measure your work as you go. Use a flexible measuring tape, rather than a ruler or metal tape measure, for a more accurate reading.

TAPESTRY NEEDLE. These needles are thick and blunt tipped, with an eye wide enough to accommodate various thicknesses of yarn. They are available in many materials, including plastic, metal, and even bone. I prefer those made of metal with a bent tip, which are available from a variety of brands.

SCISSORS OR SNIPS. I prefer to use a pair of snips with small, sharp blades for cutting yarn very accurately. They should be on hand for snipping any ends after weaving them in.

STITCH MARKERS. These are a must for marking where a round begins and ends, and where you need to work increases or decreases.

SCRAP YARN. You will need this to hold your stitches when working an optional provisional cast on (see page 117).

CABLE NEEDLE. This holds stitches when working cables. Alternatively, you can use a double-pointed needle. (I prefer using a double-pointed needle because you can knit the cable stitches straight from the needle.)

ROW COUNTER. Counting rows is a critical part of cowlette knitting. A row counter is a pocket-size device that keeps track of your rows. They come in an array of forms, from necklaces to clickers to digital apps. My favorites are the counters you can wear on your finger, like the ones shown on the opposite page.

GAUGE RULER. This is a critical tool for precise cowlette knitting because it allows you to accurately measure your swatch.

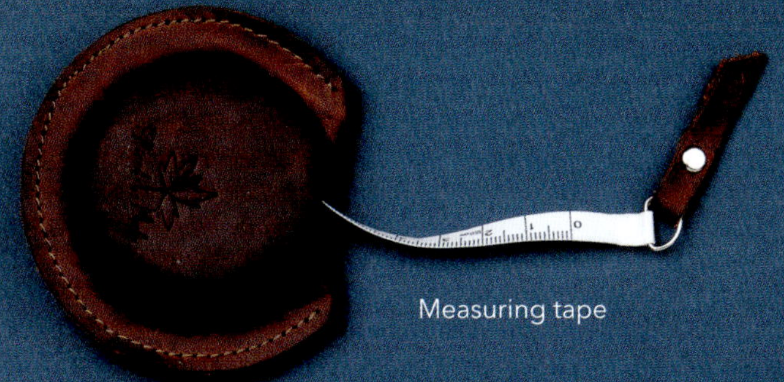
Measuring tape

Stitch markers

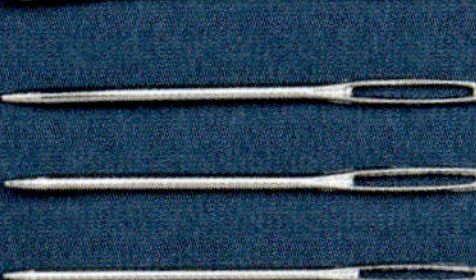
Tapestry needles

Digital row counter

Ring row counter

Snips

Cable needles

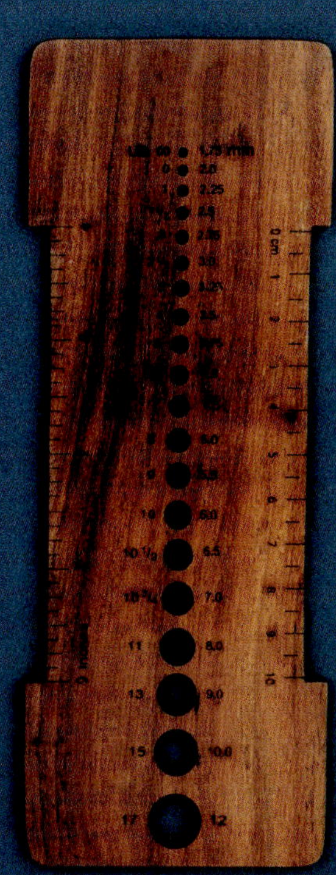
Gauge ruler

CHAPTER 2

Choose Your Path

The time has come to select a path for your cowlette adventure. In this chapter I discuss what makes a cowlette a cowlette, and walk you through all of the steps involved in knitting one. I'll also introduce you to the design decisions that you will make along the way if you plan to create custom patterns using the Cowlette Knitter's Worksheet (page 112). Not sure how to do a step? The Glossary of Techniques starting on page 116 is an additional guide to help make your journey a success.

Cowlette Knitting 101

Every pattern begins with 3 stitches. (This is one reason why cowlettes are such an easy project to get started; you don't have to cast on and count a ton of stitches.) These stitches become a small, unassuming rectangle. More rows are then added to achieve the desired neckline circumference, while strategically placed increases create the shape. As soon as the fabric is large enough to wear comfortably around your neck, it is joined in the round. From here, there are a few directions that you can go in. Want to make a smaller cowlette? Just add a decorative edge and finish with a stretchy bind off. Or, for a larger cowlette, continue the increases until it is your desired size, then add a decorative edge and bind off. On the following pages I'll teach the entire cowlette-making process, step by step.

Cowlette Shapes

There are two basic cowlette shapes in this book: triangle and half-pi. Both are very easy to execute and very wearable. They can also be combined to create a hybrid variation, such as a heart shape. The shape of your cowlette is mostly an aesthetic choice. For a complete listing of cowlette patterns by shape, see page 125.

Triangles

I have a special place in my knitty heart for triangular cowlettes. Their angular shape adds a hint of modernity to an otherwise classic knit, and I'm a sucker for mixing new and old. There are two types of triangular cowlettes: kerchiefs and ponchos.

A KERCHIEF COWLETTE has one point in the front, and the back is tailored to drape around your shoulders by working increases at the center and edges until the neckline is complete. Then the front is shaped by working 2 increases in the center of every other row until it is your desired size.

A PONCHO COWLETTE has two points: one in the front and one in the back. To create this shape, you make 4 increases every other row: one at the beginning, two in the center, and one at the end. After the work is joined in the round, you continue the increases just as before.

Worked flat, **increases** are used to reach the desired neck circumference.
Kerchief cowlettes begin with a tab **setup**, a small knitted rectangle.
Edge stitches create a neat border.
Once the work is joined in the round, center increases shape the front.
The **bind off** creates an edge with just the right amount of stretch.

Heart-shaped cowlettes blend pointed corners with the half-pi's softly rounded edges.

The semicircular half-pi cowlette boasts a simple curved shape and comfortable coverage.

ADDING MOTIFS TO TRIANGULAR COWLETTES

Because increases are so frequent in triangular cowlettes, adding motifs such as lace and cables to the mix can be tricky. The "spine," or 2 increases in the center of the triangle, produces a noticeable column of stitches that can interrupt some knitting motifs. Although you can try to incorporate the spine into lace stitch patterns by mirroring it on either side of the column, a much easier way to add cables and lace patterns to your design is to create a decorative edging. If you go this route, you can't add too much length. As a rule of thumb, I don't go over 4 inches (10 centimeters), and this tends to save me from what I call "the bunchies" or horizontal wrinkling.

Half-Pi

The half-pi is a semicircular shawl developed by knitter extraordinaire Elizabeth Zimmermann. To make this shape, start by working an increase row followed by 1 row of plain knitting. Next, work another increase row, then knit 2 rows, followed by another increase row. Then knit 4 rows plain. Do you see the pattern? After each increase row, we are doubling the number of rows of plain knitting before the next increase row.

As the piece grows, the increases become less frequent, and there are longer stretches of plain knitting, which are perfect for easily adding more complicated stitches.

Half-pi designs often have more stitches than their triangle-shaped cousins, so they require more yarn and take longer to knit.

Hybrids

Once you understand the fundamentals of triangular and half-pi shaping, you can move on to experimenting with increases to create more shapes.

HEART SHAPE. My favorite hybrid is the heart-shaped cowlette. It has the sharp corners of a triangle and the rounded edge of a half-pi, and it curves very delicately around the wearer's neck.

The heart shape begins as an unassuming triangle, with increases worked on every right-side row: 2 increases at the beginning of the row, 2 in the center, and 2 at the end, for a total of 6 increases per increase row. The next wrong-side row is then worked even. Increase and plain rows are then alternated until the cowlette is your desired size.

Setups

Once you cast on 3 stitches, it is time to set up your cowlette. A setup allows you to increase the cowlette size without warping the fabric. If you increase randomly, or simply cast on more stitches, the fabric just won't lie flat.

There are two types of setups in this book—the increase setup and the tab setup—both of which can be done in garter or stockinette stitch. The increase setup adds in more stitches with strategic increases. The tab setup has you knit a tiny rectangle and then pick up more stitches along the longer side. Although each pattern tells you which setup to use, I've outlined below how to execute both, for my adventurous friends who might want to switch things up.

Here I will explain each type, the best time to use them, and teach you how to make them with step-by-step instructions. Feel free to follow along with some scrap yarn and needles.

When working any setup, I recommend starting with a long-tail cast on (see page 116). It creates a first row that is moderately stretchy, which is perfect for a neck opening. The correct setup for each design is also included in the patterns in Chapter 3.

Increase Setups

Increase setups are my favorite because they are quick and no fuss, allowing you to get to knitting faster. The only downside to this type of setup is that it creates a little dip in the center, for a slight crescent shape. Although the dip is not very noticeable when worn, some of my more particular friends may not like it. (If you prefer to not have a dip, skip to the tab setups on page 32.)

INCREASE SETUP IN GARTER STITCH. This setup is for cowlettes with a stockinette- or garter-stitch body. The squishy and compact garter stitch prevents the edges of your work from rolling. (Don't know how to make a kfb increase? Turn to page 120.)

Using the long-tail method, cast on 3 stitches.

Row 1 (RS): (Kfb) twice, k1; 5 sts.

Row 2 (WS): Knit.

Row 3: (Kfb) 4 times, k1; 9 sts.

Row 4: Knit.

INCREASE SETUP IN STOCKINETTE STITCH. This setup works best when the body of the cowlette is in garter stitch or a pattern that incorporates garter stitch. The edge rolls very neatly into itself, creating a straight contrasting edge, which matches my all-time favorite bind off for cowlettes, Jeny's Surprisingly Stretchy Bind Off (see page 119). I do not recommend using it on a stockinette body because the rolled edge takes over and can cause the whole project to roll.

Using the long-tail method, cast on 3 stitches.

Row 1 (RS): (Kfb) twice, k1; 5 sts.
Row 2 (WS): Purl.
Row 3: (Kfb) 4 times, k1; 9 sts.
Row 4: Purl.

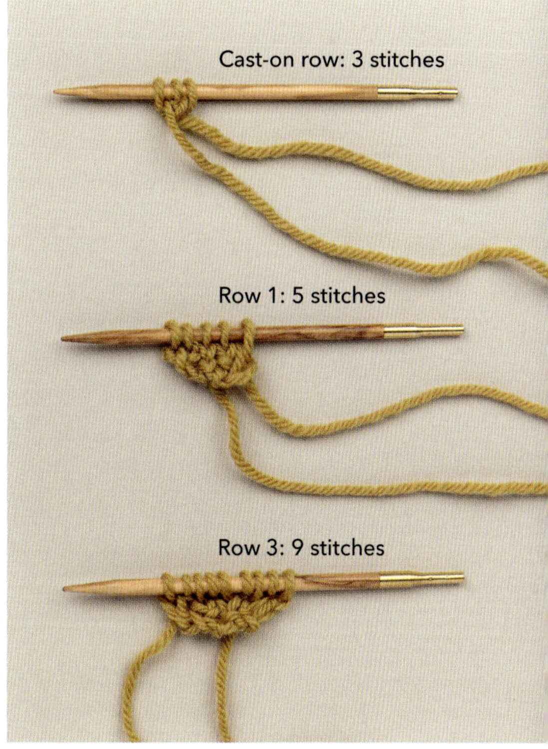

A MYSTERIOUS HUMP

Sometimes when working setup rows, you will notice a mysterious hump at the top of the cowlette. This is completely normal for top-down cowlette shaping, so no worries! Going up a needle size will help put some space in between the stitches and give them a place to relax once the cowlette is blocked.

Tab Setups

A tab setup is a little rectangle that becomes the top center of a cowlette. Unlike increase setups, which have a slight dip, tab setups are straight across.

GARTER TAB. Just like the increase setup in garter stitch, I recommend using the garter tab on cowlettes with a stockinette body to prevent the work from curling. It can also be used on cowlettes with a garter body. Note: All even rows are RS rows.

Using the long-tail method, cast on 3 stitches.

Rows 1-7: Knit; do not turn after Row 7. Now, you will pick up stitches knitwise. The easiest way to do this is to pick up and knit 3 stitches along the edge of the knitting, then pick up and knit 3 stitches along the cast-on edge. You should now have 9 stitches on your needle. Turn to work a RS row.

STOCKINETTE TAB. The stockinette tab is worked the same way as a garter tab, but it's knit in stockinette. And just like with the increase setup in stockinette, stockinette tabs are great for cowlettes with garter stitch bodies. Just note that it will not prevent stockinette-bodied cowlettes from rolling onto themselves. It is also a perfect complement to Jeny's Surprisingly Stretchy Bind Off (see page 119).

Using the long tail method, cast on 3 stitches.

Rows 1-7: Beginning with a purl row (WS), work in stockinette; do not turn after Row 7. Now, you will pick up stitches purlwise. The easiest way to do this is to pick up (but do not knit!) 3 stitches alongside the edge of the knitting, then pick up 3 stitches along the cast-on edge. You should now have 9 stitches on your needle. Turn to work a RS row.

TRY A PROVISIONAL CAST ON

For an even smoother appearance, start tab setups with a provisional cast on. With a provisional cast on, you create the initial stitches on a scrap of waste yarn. So, instead of picking up stitches along the cast-on edge, you simply pull out the scrap yarn to reveal live stitches that are ready to be slipped to your left needle and worked in pattern. Check out page 117 for the easiest version of the provisional cast on, the long-tail provisional cast on.

GARTER TAB SETUP

Step 1. Cast on 3 stitches. (We've used the long-tail cast on method, but most cast ons should be fine!)

Step 2. Knit 7 rows in garter stitch. This creates 3 sets of garter bumps.

Step 3. Rotate piece 90 degrees clockwise. Pick up 3 stitches down the side, 1 in each garter bump.

Step 4. Knit the 3 stitches you picked up. *6 stitches total.*

Step 5. Now rotate piece another 90 degrees clockwise and pick up 3 stitches in the cast-on edge. This can be tricky; you could just pick up the left strand of each cast-on stitch.

Step 6. Knit the 3 stitches you picked up. You now have 9 stitches and are ready to knit that cowlette! Turn to work a RS row.

How to Calculate Neck Opening

Now that you know the various shapes and setup stitches, it's time to learn how to calculate the number of rows you need to work the neck opening to the desired size. This is easy to do, thanks to the following formula:

[Rows per inch (or rows per centimeter) × desired circumference – setup rows] ÷ 4

Multiply the rows per inch (or per centimeter) by the desired neck opening circumference, then subtract the number of setup rows and divide by four. If you happen to get a decimal, round up or down to an odd number.

For example, the Journey cowlette on page 51 has 6 rows per inch (2.4 rows per centimeter) × a 22.5 inch (56.5 centimeter) circumference – 7 stockinette tab setup rows ÷ by 4 = 32 rows.

Thirty-two rows would have left me on the wrong side row, so I worked a total of thirty-one rows before joining in the round on the right side of the cowlette.

Choosing a Size

I live in the windy Midwest, so I prefer a narrow, neck warmer–style cowlette that is 18–20 inches (45–50 centimeters) around to help keep the chilly air out. On warmer days, I like to wear larger, drapey standard-size cowlettes, which are approximately 22–24 inches (55–60 centimeters) around.

ADDING STITCH PATTERNS TO THE MIX

A stitch motif is a collection of stitches that creates a particular surface pattern that is repeated over a specific number of stitches. For example, in the US, moss stitch is worked over 2 stitches, so the total stitch count will need to be a multiple of 2. These numbers are approximate and can be adjusted. Although I try not to take away rows, I may add a few to fit in another increase row to finish a motif, just because I like the way it looks. Just note that this will affect the final neck opening. Luckily, cowlettes are very forgiving. This is why the Half-Pi Cowlette has a slightly bigger neck opening than the Triangle Cowlette. I really wanted to squeeze in another row of yarnover increases, simply because I liked the way they looked.

Edge Stitches

Edge stitches are one of the most important parts of cowlette knitting. They keep the edges stable and looking nice and neat, and in the end they frame the face of the wearer. In each pattern there are a total of 6 edge stitches: 3 at the beginning and 3 at the end. Ultimately, they will make up the bulk of the cowlette's neckline. Feel free to add more than 6 edge stitches to your own designs, but I wouldn't recommend having any fewer. You really need at least 3 on each end to create a stable edge.

OPPOSITES ATTRACT

In the patterns you will notice that the stockinette cowlettes have a garter edge and that the garter cowlettes have a stockinette edge. When paired with garter stitch, the stockinette edge rolls into itself and creates a clean line that is reminiscent of an I-cord. Also, a stockinette cowlette needs a garter edge to prevent the entire cowlette from rolling. Whichever edge you choose, make sure that the body is worked in a different stitch and place stitch markers inside each set of edge stitches as a reminder to work in the established pattern. (You can, of course, make an entire project in garter like Li'l One on page 91, and the edges will lie perfectly flat. But you will lose my favorite part: the frame!)

Shaping Increases

Now that you have an understanding of cowlette shapes and setups, it's time to pick an increase type to help shape your cowlette.

When knitting a triangular cowlette, you add 4 stitches every other row (one at the start of the row, two in the middle of the row, and one at the end). This will create a symmetrical triangle that will grow larger incrementally.

Increases for a half-pi cowlette take a more horizontal approach. Instead of increasing steadily every other row, you work an expanding sequence. On increase rows, you double (or double plus one) the stitches inside the edges. Then you work rows of plain knitting, doubling the number of plain rows that were worked before the last increase row. Continuing this sequence will create a nearly perfect semicircle.

Types of Increases

Now that we have some stitches on our needles, let's work on increasing them to create a cowlette that can go around your neck. Below you will find the four different types of increases used in this book. New to making increases? Turn to the Glossary of Techniques on page 116 for step-by-step instructions.

KNIT-FRONT-AND-BACK (KFB). The kfb is a quick and simple option that's perfect for beginners and is often one of the first increases knitters learn. It blends beautifully into garter stitch, but in stockinette it creates a small, visible bump in your knitting. Some people may consider this a disruption, but I think the little bumps create a cute design element, and I still use kfb in stockinette all the time.

KNIT-FRONT-SLIP-BACK (KFSB). The kfsb increase was popularized by Staci Perry of VeryPink Knits. It is similar to kfb, with the only difference being that we are slipping the back of the stitch purlwise instead of knitting into it. This eliminates the bump that knitting into the back of a stitch can create, making this option appear smoother. And it's still as quick and easy as the kfb.

YARNOVER (YO). Yarnover increases work with all gauges and stitch motifs, will always look symmetrical, and are super easy to do.

MAKE 1 RIGHT AND MAKE 1 LEFT (M1R AND M1L). This one is for all the perfectionists out there. These two increases allow triangular cowlettes to look symmetrical and will make half-pi cowlette increases seem invisible.

When to Use Knit-Front-and-Back (Kfb) and Knit-Front-Slip-Back (Kfsb)

I grouped kfb and kfsb together because they are very similar and are used in most of the same situations. I prefer to use them in cowlettes that feature a lot of stockinette and garter. When paired with textured or lace stitches, the kfb and kfsb increases can be quite visible. And that is perfectly fine. It's up to you whether you want the increases to be seen.

When to Use Yarnover (Yo)

The yarnover is the only increase that works in literally any cowlette style, and it really shines in lacy designs. The yarnover creates a little hole in your knitting. It not only matches the lacy motifs aesthetically, the extra air adds to the drape of the finished cowlette. So, if you are looking for a cowlette that will feel as light and airy as the wind around your neck, try the yarnover increase.

When to Use Make 1 Right (M1r) and Make 1 Left (M1l)

M1r and m1l are directional increases that lean to the right or to the left, respectively. For example, if you want to place an increase to the left of the edge stitches, then you will work a m1l. The same rule applies for the m1r. If you are a fan of symmetry and order, and are willing to do a touch of fiddling, then I highly recommend this increase pair. When using these increases in a half-pi cowlette, be sure to pick either a m1r or a m1l to be used for the entirety of the project. For half-pi cowlettes, consistency is more important than the actual direction of the increase.

Cowlette Depth

Cowlette depth is the vertical measurement taken from the cast on to the bind off. Although this measurement is completely up to you, you may want to take a look at the pattern photos and finished depth to see how each looks when worn. Alternatively, you can take on my favorite approach to depth, which is "knit in pattern until you have just enough yarn to bind off."

ADDING STYLE WITH FANCY STITCHES

Cowlettes don't necessarily need intricate stitches or fancy edges to look good. They are perfect as is, when knit in a basic garter stitch with a simple bind off. But even though they don't need to be dressed up, adding a little flourish is a good thing! In the patterns, you will see several examples of how to add something extra to your cowlette. Whether it's textured stitches, cables, or just a fancy bind off, there are lots of options for dressing up a cowlette.

The picot bind off adds visual appeal and creates a stretchy edge that allows knitting to lie flat.

Binding Off

Picking the right bind off is critical. Between the looser gauge and the pizzazz stitches like lace patterns and cables, you really need to choose a bind off that has a bit of stretch to avoid puckering. Turn to the Glossary of Techniques on page 116 for step-by-step instructions.

JENY'S SURPRISINGLY STRETCHY BIND OFF. This is my preferred bind off because it is so versatile, quick, and easy to work. It is also truly "surprisingly stretchy," ensuring that your stitches will lie flat. It has a different effect on the final look of your project, depending on which side you work it. On the right side, it will blend in beautifully with garter or purl stitches. Worked on the wrong side, it produces an edge of stockinette stitches that will match any of the stockinette setups perfectly.

PICOT BIND OFF. I love a picot bind off. If you are looking for an easy, stretchy bind off that can be applied to pretty much any pattern and will add a tasteful bit of pizzazz, then look no further. I am slightly embarrassed about how often I put picots in my work. But I truly believe that there is nothing more graceful than a plain stockinette project finished with a delicate row of picots.

Picots appear in an array of handicrafts, from bobbin lace to crochet. In knitting, *picot* (which means "small point" in French) is typically used to describe any set of mountain-like peaks that are formed along a knitted edge. They can appear vertically or horizontally and are created by adding stitches, usually with increases or a cast on, then sharply decreasing the added stitches via a bind off. This can be done on a vertical edge of a piece of knitting (similar to Betrothed on page 103), or horizontally as a bind off.

Because we are adding stitches, the picot bind off is naturally stretchy, allowing delicate lace stitches to lie nice and flat.

This version of the picot bind off is often worked on a multiple of three stitches, but this is flexible. You can also cast on more stitches for taller picots or adjust the spacing between the picots by adding or subtracting the number of stitches bound off. The more stitches that are bound off, the more spaced out the picots will be.

Since a cowlette is worked in the round, once you run out of stitches to bind off, run the tail through the last stitch and use that tail to tack both ends of the picot together.

Tips for Customizing Your Cowlette

When you feel ready to embark on creating your own design from scratch, here are a few math tips to guide you through the process. The beauty of the cowlette is that you can easily adjust the stitch counts to fit whatever motif you want. Trust me, no one will notice! There are just a couple of rules to follow to help you execute this smoothly.

INCREASE AND DECREASE WISELY. In most cases, I highly recommend increasing rather than decreasing stitches to reach a desired stitch count, to avoid making a cowlette that is too small. If, however, you have one or two stitches too many for a motif, simply decrease them evenly across the next row or round. Just keep in mind that if you're working with a super bulky yarn, like with Ashes on page 47, two stitches can equal more than a whole inch, a decrease that could lead to a tighter, neck warmer–style cowlette that is too snug to enjoy!

YOU DON'T NEED TO WORK AROUND INCREASES. If you want to take things as easy as possible, you technically don't need to try to fit your favorite motif around the cowlette "spine" (the column of increases on triangle and hybrid designs). You can just begin the motif whenever you are ready and work even in that pattern. Though this will create a less defined shape, it's still one of my favorite ways to whip up a quick cowlette.

CHAPTER 3

The Cowlette Patterns

Now that you've learned all of the steps, it's time for the fun part: making cowlettes! I have created 23 patterns for you to knit, wear, gift, and love. The yarn and exact techniques used in each pattern are listed for your convenience. But remember: You are the boss of your knitting! If you wish to forgo the garter and stockinette tabs and work an easier increase setup instead, that's perfectly fine. I do not recommend, however, changing the shape because this can affect the stitch counts. Keep a triangle a triangle and a half-pi a half-pi, and the rest is fair game. I also highly recommend that you begin with one of the first two patterns, The Triangle or The Half-Pi, before jumping into the more complex designs.

THE TRIANGLE

This quintessential triangle-shaped cowlette features a garter stitch body, a stockinette edge, and a column of slipped stitches down the center.

FINISHED MEASUREMENTS

(After Blocking)

- Neck Opening: 20" (50 cm)
- Depth: 12½" (31.5 cm)

SHAPE

- Triangle (Kerchief)

GAUGE

- 16 sts and 28 rows/rounds = 4" (10 cm) in garter stitch

YARN

- Kelbourne Woolens Germantown, 100% North American wool, worsted, 220 yds/201 m (100 g), 1 skein in 708 Honey

NEEDLES

- US 9 (5.5 mm) circular needles in 24" (60 cm) and 32" (80 cm) lengths or size needed to obtain gauge

NOTIONS

- 4 stitch markers

SETUP AND INCREASE

Using shorter needles, begin with a Stockinette Tab (page 32); 9 sts. As your cowlette grows, switch to longer needles.

Row 1 (Increase Row Setup, RS): K3, pm, m1l, k1, m1r, pm, k1, pm, m1l, k1, m1r, pm, k3; 13 sts.

Row 2 (WS): P3, sm, k to m, sm, sl1 wyif, sm, k to m, sm, p3.

Row 3 (Increase Row): K3, sm, m1l, k to m, m1r, sm, k1, sm, m1l, k to m, m1r, sm, k3; 4 sts increased.

Row 4 (and every WS row): P3, sm, k to m, sm, sl1 wyif, sm, k to m, sm, p3.

Rows 5-40: Repeat Rows 3 & 4 eighteen times more; 89 sts.

Row 41 (Increase Row): Work Row 3 once more, removing the first and last stitch marker, do not turn work; 93 sts.

JOIN IN THE ROUND

Using backward loop method, cast on 1 stitch, pm for BOR and join to work in the round; 94 sts.

Round 1 (RS): P to m, sm, sl1 wyib, sm, p to end of round.

Round 2 (Increase Round): K to m, m1r, sm, k1, sm, m1l, k to end of round; 2 sts increased.

Rounds 3-28: Repeat Rounds 1 & 2 thirteen times more; 122 sts.

Turn work so that WS is facing.

Work Jeny's Surprisingly Stretchy Bind Off (page 119).

FINISHING

Cut yarn; weave in ends. Block to measurements.

THE HALF-PI

Designed to be The Triangle's counterpart, The Half-Pi features a simple, rounded design that can be paired with anything!

FINISHED MEASUREMENTS
(After Blocking)

- Neck Opening: 22" (55 cm)
- Depth: 13" (32.5 cm)

SHAPE

- Half-Pi

GAUGE

- 16 sts and 28 rows/rounds = 4" (10 cm) in garter stitch

YARN

- Kelbourne Woolens Germantown, 100% North American wool, worsted, 220 yds/201 m (100 g), 1 skein in 340 Sage

NEEDLES

- US 9 (5.5 mm) circular needles in 24" (60 cm) and 32" (80 cm) lengths or size needed to obtain gauge

NOTIONS

- 2 stitch markers

SETUP AND INCREASE

Using shorter needles, begin with Increase Setup in Stockinette Stitch (page 31); 9 sts. As your cowlette grows, switch to longer needles.

Row 1 (Increase Row Setup, RS): K3, pm, [yo, k1] 3 times, yo, pm, k3; 13 sts.

Row 2 (WS): P3, sm, k to m, sm, p3.

Row 3: Knit, slipping markers.

Row 4 (and every WS row): P3, sm, k to m, sm, p3.

Row 5 (Increase Row): K3, sm, [yo, k1] to m, yo, sm, k3; 21 sts.

Row 6: WS row.

Rows 7-10: Repeat Rows 3 & 4 twice more.

Row 11 (Increase Row): Same as Row 5; 37 sts.

Row 12: WS row.

Rows 13-20: Repeat Rows 3 & 4 four times.

Row 21 (Increase Row): Same as Row 5; 69 sts.

Row 22: WS Row.

Rows 23-38: Repeat Rows 3 & 4 eight times.

Row 39 (Increase Row): Same as Row 5; 133 sts.

Row 40: WS row.

Row 41: Knit, removing markers, do not turn work.

JOIN IN THE ROUND

Using backward loop method, cast on 1 st, pm for BOR and join to work in the round; 134 sts.

Round 1 (RS): Purl.

Round 2: Knit.

Round 3: Purl.

Rounds 4–35: Repeat Rounds 2 & 3 sixteen times.

Round 36 (Increase Round): [Yo, k1] to end of round; 268 sts.

Round 37: Purl.

Turn work so that WS is facing.

Work Jeny's Surprisingly Stretchy Bind Off (page 119).

FINISHING

Cut yarn; weave in ends. Block to measurements.

ASHES

Ashes was designed to be a modern response to a poncho. Knitted in a cool neutral, Ashes elevates your day-to-day outfit while keeping the chill off your neck.

FINISHED MEASUREMENTS

(After Blocking)

- Neck Opening: 25" (62.5 cm)
- Depth: 21" (52.5 cm)

SHAPE

- Triangle (Kerchief)

GAUGE

- 7 sts and 10 rows/rounds = 4" (10 cm) in stockinette stitch

YARN

- Rowan BIG Big Wool, 100% merino wool, super bulky, 44 yds/40 m (100 g), 3 balls in Fossil 212

NEEDLES

- US 17 (12 mm) circular needles in 24" (60 cm) and 32" (80 cm) lengths or size needed to obtain gauge

NOTIONS

- 4 stitch markers

SETUP AND INCREASE

Using shorter needles, begin with a Garter Tab (page 32); 9 sts. As your cowlette grows, switch to longer needles.

Row 1 (Increase Row Setup, RS): K3, pm, m1l, k1, m1r, pm, k1, pm, m1l, k1, m1r, pm, k3; 13 sts.

Row 2 (WS): K3, sm, p to m, sm, sl1 wyif, sm, p to m, sm, k3.

Row 3 (Increase Row): K3, sm, m1l, k to m, m1r, sm, k1, sm, m1l, k to m, m1r, sm, k3; 4 sts increased.

Row 4 (and every WS row): K3, sm, p to m, sm, sl1 wyif, sm, p to m, sm, k3.

Rows 5-20: Repeat Rows 3 & 4 eight times more; 49 sts.

Row 21 (Increase Row): Work Row 3 once more, removing the first and last stitch marker, do not turn work; 53 sts.

JOIN IN THE ROUND

Using backward loop method, cast on 1 stitch, pm for BOR and join to work in the round; 54 sts.

Round 1 (RS): K to m, sm, sl1 wyib, sm, k to end of round.

Round 2 (Increase Round): K to m, m1r, sm, k1, sm, m1l, k to end of round; 2 sts increased.

Rounds 3-14: Repeat Rounds 1 & 2 six times more; 68 sts.

Round 15: Purl, slipping markers.

Round 16 (Increase Round): Same as Round 2; 70 sts.

Rounds 17 & 18: Repeat Rounds 15 & 16 once more; 72 sts.

Turn work so that WS is facing.

Work Jeny's Surprisingly Stretchy Bind Off (page 119).

FINISHING

Cut yarn; weave in ends. Block to measurements.

JOURNEY

Journey was inspired by the hero's tale, the wandering cable representing the meandering stories of our favorite odysseys.

FINISHED MEASUREMENTS

(After Blocking)

- Neck Opening: 22½" (56.5 cm)
- Depth: 19" (47.5 cm)

SHAPE

- Triangle (Kerchief)

GAUGE

- 16 sts and 24 rows/rounds = 4" (10 cm) in garter stitch

YARN

- Blue Sky Fibers Woolstok Tweed, 85% Fine Highland wool/15% Donegal, Aran, 109 yds/100 m (100 g), 1 hank each in 3307 Fern Frond (Color A) and 3312 Sage Rose (Color B)

NEEDLES

- US 11 (8 mm) circular needles in 24" (60 cm) and 32" (80 cm) lengths or size needed to obtain gauge

NOTIONS

- Cable needle, 4 stitch markers

SETUP AND INCREASE

Using shorter needles and Color A, begin with a Stockinette Tab (page 32); 9 sts. As your cowlette grows, switch to longer needles.

Row 1 (Increase Setup Row, RS): K3, pm, m1l, k1, m1r, pm, k1, pm, m1l, k1, m1r, pm, k3; 13 sts.

Row 2 (WS): P3, sm, k to m, sm, sl1 wyif, sm, k to m, sm, p3.

Row 3 (Increase Row): K3, sm, m1l, k to m, m1r, sm, k1, sm, m1l, k to m, m1r, sm, k3; 4 sts increased.

Row 4 (and every WS Row): P3, sm, k to m, sm, sl1 wyif, sm, k to m, sm, p3.

Rows 5-30: Repeat Rows 3 & 4 thirteen times more; 69 sts.

Row 31 (Increase Row): Work Row 3 once more, removing the first and last stitch marker, do not turn work; 73 sts.

JOIN IN THE ROUND

Using backward loop method, cast on 1 st, pm for BOR and join to work in the round; 74 sts.

Round 1 (RS): P to m, sm, sl1 wyib, sm, p to end of round.

Round 2 (Increase Round): K to m, m1r, sm, k1, sm, m1l, k to end of round; 2 sts increased.

Rounds 3–16: Repeat Rounds 1 & 2 seven times more; 90 sts.

Rounds 17 & 18: Using Color B, repeat Rounds 1 & 2 once more; 92 sts.

Rounds 19 & 20: Using Color A, repeat Rounds 1 & 2 once more; 94 sts. Remove BOR marker. Do not turn work.

Cut Color A.

Sideways Braid

Using Color B and cable method, cast on 11 sts to the left needle.

You will now work perpendicular to your knitting to create a sideways braid. Every right-side row will end with an ssk, which is worked with 1 braid stitch and 1 stitch from the cowlette body.

Using the chart or written instructions, work Rows 1–8 twenty-three times, then repeat Rows 1–5 once more, until all body stitches are consumed.

JOURNEY CHART WRITTEN INSTRUCTIONS

Row 1 (RS): K9, p1, ssk, turn work.

Row 2 (and every WS row): Sl1 wyif, k1, p9.

Row 3: K3, C6B, p1, ssk, turn work.

Row 4: WS Row.

Row 5: Same as Row 1.

Row 6: WS Row.

Row 7: C6F, k3, p1, ssk, turn work.

Row 8: WS Row.

Using a regular bind off, bind off in pattern.

FINISHING

Block to measurements, then use mattress stitch to seam the cast on to the bind off (page 122).

Cut yarn; weave in ends.

JOURNEY CHART

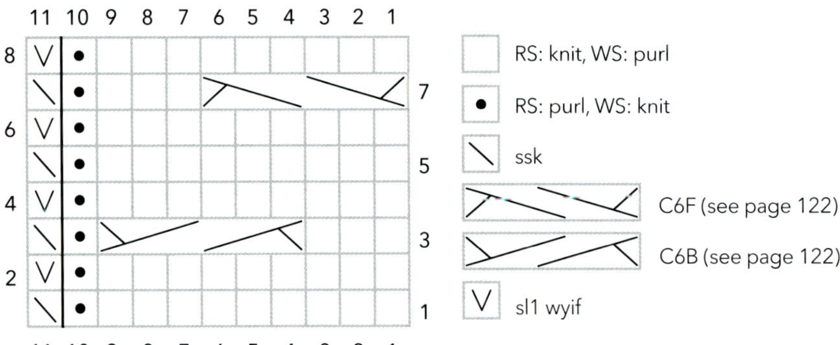

RESPITE

Shorter and a bit more graceful than Journey, Respite is what I imagine the hero wore after returning home safely.

FINISHED MEASUREMENTS

(After Blocking)

- Neck Opening: 21" (52.5 cm)
- Depth: 12¼" (30.5 cm)

SHAPE

- Half-Pi

GAUGE

- 16 sts and 24 rows/rounds = 4" (10 cm) in garter stitch

YARN

- Blue Sky Fibers Woolstok Tweed, 85% Fine Highland wool/15% Donegal, Aran, 109 yds/100 m (100 g), 1 hank each in 3312 Sage Rose (Color A) and 3307 Fern Frond (Color B)

NEEDLES

- US 11 (8 mm) circular needles in 24" (60 cm) length or size needed to obtain gauge

NOTIONS

- Cable needle, 2 stitch markers

SETUP AND INCREASE

Using Color A, begin with a Stockinette Tab (page 32); 9 sts.

Row 1 (Increase Setup Row, RS): K3, pm, [yo, k1] 3 times, yo, pm, k3; 13 sts.

Row 2 (WS): P3, sm, k to m, sm, p3.

Row 3: Knit, slipping markers.

Row 4 (and every WS row): P3, sm, k to m, sm, p3.

Row 5 (Increase Row): K3, sm, [yo, k1] to m, yo, sm, k3; 21 sts.

Row 6: WS row.

Rows 7-10: Repeat Rows 3 & 4 twice more.

Row 11 (Increase Row): Same as Row 5; 37 sts.

Row 12: WS row.

Rows 13-20: Repeat Rows 3 & 4 four times more.

Row 21 (Increase Row): Same as Row 5; 69 sts.

Row 22: WS row.

Rows 23-28: Repeat Rows 3 & 4 three times more.

Row 29: Knit, removing markers, do not turn work.

JOIN IN THE ROUND

Using backward loop method, cast on 1 stitch, pm for BOR and join to work in the round; 70 sts.

Round 1 (RS): Purl.

Round 2: Knit.

Round 3: Purl.

Rounds 4-7: Repeat Rounds 2 & 3 twice more.

Rounds 8 & 9: Using Color B, repeat Rounds 2 & 3 once more.

Rounds 10 & 11: Using Color A, repeat Rounds 2 & 3 once more. Remove BOR marker. Do not turn work.

Cut Color A.

RESPITE CHART

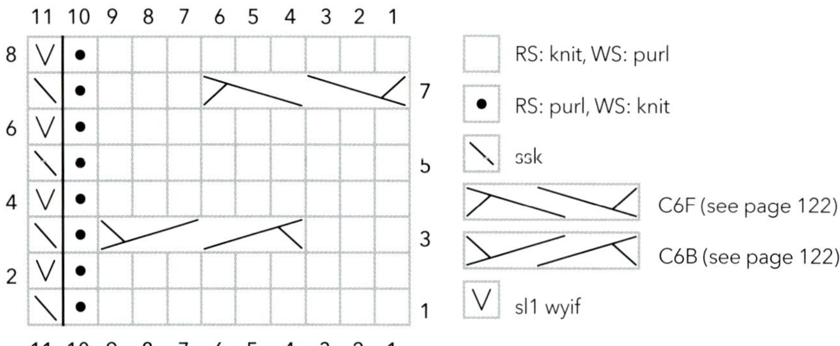

Sideways Braid

Using Color B and cable method, cast on 11 sts to the left needle.

You will now work perpendicular to your knitting to create a sideways braid. Every right-side row will end with an ssk, which is worked with 1 braid stitch and 1 stitch from the cowlette body.

Using the chart or written instructions, work Rows 1–8 seventeen times, then work Rows 1–5 once more until all body stitches are consumed.

RESPITE CHART WRITTEN INSTRUCTIONS

Row 1 (RS): K9, p1, ssk, turn work.

Row 2 (and every WS row): Sl1 wyif, k1, p9.

Row 3: K3, C6B, p1, ssk, turn work.

Row 4: WS Row.

Row 5: Same as Row 1.

Row 6: WS Row.

Row 7: C6F, k3, p1, ssk, turn work.

Row 8: WS Row.

Using a regular bind off, bind off in pattern.

FINISHING

Block to measurements. Use mattress stitch to seam the cast on to the bind off (page 122).

Cut yarn; weave in ends.

MIST

Mist marries a robust Aran weight yarn with a wispy, lighter-than-air mohair lace to create a unique fabric filled with texture and drape.

FINISHED MEASUREMENTS (After Blocking)

- Neck Opening: 18" (45 cm)
- Depth: 24" (60 cm)

SHAPE

- Triangle (Kerchief)

GAUGE

- 18 sts and 32 rows/rounds = 4" (10 cm) in Stripe Pattern

YARN

- Rowan Kidsilk Haze, 70% mohair/30% silk, lace, 229 yds/210 m (25 g), 1 ball in Pearl 590 (Color A)
- Rowan Kid Classic, 70% wool/22% mohair/ 8% polyamide, Aran, 153 yds/140 m (50 g), 1 ball in Bittersweet 866 (Color B)

NEEDLES

- US 8 (5 mm) circular needles in 16" (40 cm) and 24" (60 cm) lengths or size needed to obtain gauge

NOTIONS

- 4 stitch markers

Stripe Pattern Flat

Row 1 (RS): Using Color A, knit.

Row 2 (WS): Using Color A, purl.

Row 3: Same as Row 1.

Row 4: Same as Row 2.

Row 5: Using Color B, knit.

Row 6: Using Color B, knit.

Stripe Pattern in the Round

Rounds 1–4: Using Color A, knit.

Round 5: Using Color B, knit.

Round 6: Using Color B, purl.

Yarn Management Tips

When working the Stripe Pattern, there are two options for yarn management. You can cut Color B at every color change to keep that delightful misty appearance (as shown in the sample above), or you can carry Color B behind your work. Either is perfectly fine! Regardless, Color A is so light that it can be discreetly carried behind your work.

SETUP AND INCREASE

Using shorter needles and Color B, begin with Increase Setup in Garter Stitch (page 30); 9 sts. As your cowlette grows, switch to longer needles.

Row 1 (Increase Row Setup, RS): K2, [kfb] twice, k1, [kfb] twice, k2; 13 sts.

Row 2 (Marker Placement, WS): P3, pm, p3, pm, p1, pm, p3, pm, p3. Join Color A.

Row 3 (Increase Row): Working in Stripe Pattern Flat, work to m, sm, kfb, work to 1 st before m, kfb, sm, work 1 st, sm, kfb, work to 1 st before m, kfb, sm, work to end; 4 sts increased.

Row 4: Work in Stripe Pattern Flat, slipping markers.

Rows 5-44: Repeat Rows 3 & 4 twenty times more; 97 sts.

On last row, remove the first and last stitch marker, do not turn work.

JOIN IN THE ROUND

Using backward loop method, cast on 1 stitch, pm for BOR and join to work in the round; 98 sts.

Round 1 (Increase Round, RS): Working in Stripe Pattern in the Round, work to m, m1r, sm, work 1 st, sm, m1l, work to end of round; 2 sts increased.

Round 2: Working in Stripe Pattern in the Round, work to m, sm, work to end of round.

Rounds 3-72: Repeat Rounds 1 & 2 thirty-five times more; 170 sts. End with Round 6 of Stripe Pattern in the Round.

Work Jeny's Surprisingly Stretchy Bind Off (page 119).

FINISHING

Cut yarn; weave in ends. Block to measurements.

ADDING TEXTURE BY MIXING GAUGES

I love mixing yarns of different gauges in cowlette knitting because it adds texture without much fuss. When choosing needles for a mixed gauge project, I like to go with the middle ground. In this pattern, I use Rowan Kid Classic, which calls for US 8-9 (5-5.5 mm) and Rowan Kid Silk Haze, which calls for US 3-8 (3.25-5 mm). So, for this pattern, I chose US 8 (5 mm) needles to swatch with, because that is the needle size the yarns have in common.

SEA GLASS

Have you ever seen an artfully dyed skein of yarn and thought, "I could just wear this as is?" Sea Glass was designed to look just like the skein it is knit from. This cowlette gathers at the neck when worn, creating layers of watercolor fabric. The motifs are simple because mohair can be tricky to work with, and the evenly placed purl ridges break up color pooling.

FINISHED MEASUREMENTS
(After Blocking)

- Neck Opening: 24" (60 cm)
- Depth: 24" (60 cm)

SHAPE

- Triangle (Kerchief)

GAUGE

- 24 sts and 32 rows/rounds = 4" (10 cm) in garter ridge stitch

YARN

- Neighborhood Fiber Co. Loft, 70% mohair/30% silk, lace, 459 yds/420 m (50 g), 1 skein in Rock Creek Park

NEEDLES

- US 7 (4.5 mm) circular needles in 24" (60 cm) and 32" (80 cm) lengths or size needed to obtain gauge

NOTIONS

- 4 stitch markers

Special Stitches

Elongated Stitch (kw2): Knit 1 stitch wrapping the yarn twice around the needle. On the next row/round, drop the extra wrap, creating an elongated stitch.

Garter Ridge Stitch:

Row 1 (RS): Knit.

Row 2 (WS): Purl.

Row 3: Knit.

Row 4: Knit.

SETUP AND INCREASE

Using shorter needles, begin with Increase Setup in Stockinette Stitch (page 31); 9 sts. As your cowlette grows, switch to longer needles.

Row 1 (Increase Row Setup, RS): K3, pm, yo, k1, yo, pm, k1, pm, yo, k1, yo, pm, k3; 13 sts.

Row 2 (WS): P3, sm, k to m, sm, sl1 wyif, sm, k to m, sm, p3.

Row 3 (Increase Row): K3, sm, yo, k to m, yo, sm, k1, sm, yo, k to m, yo, sm, k3; 4 sts increased.

Row 4: P3, sm, p to m, sm, sl1 wyif, sm, p to m, sm, p3.

Row 5 (Increase Row): Same as Row 3; 21 sts.

Row 6: P3, k to m, sm, sl1 wyif, sm, k to m, sm, p3.

Rows 7-50: Repeat Rows 3–6 eleven times more; 109 sts.

Row 51 (Increase Row): Work Row 3 once more, removing the first and last stitch marker, do not turn work; 113 sts.

JOIN IN THE ROUND

Using backward loop method, cast on 1 stitch, pm for BOR and join to work in the round; 114 sts.

Round 1 (RS): K to m, sm, sl1 wyib, sm, k to end of round.

Round 2 (Increase Round): K to m, yo, sm, k1, sm, yo, k to end of round; 2 sts increased.

Round 3: P to m, sm, sl1 wyib, sm, p to end of round.

Round 4 (Increase Round): K to m, yo, sm, k1, sm, yo, k to end of round; 2 sts increased.

Round 5: Kw2 to m, sm, sl1 wyib, sm, kw2 to end of round.

Round 6 (Increase Round): Dropping extra wraps from kw2 in previous round, k to m, yo, sm, k1, sm, yo, k to end of round; 2 sts increased.

Round 7: P to m, sm, sl1 wyib, sm, p to end of round.

Round 8 (Increase Round): Same as Round 4; 2 sts increased.

Round 9: K to m, sm, sl1 wyib, sm, k to end of round.

Round 10 (Increase Round): Same as Round 4; 2 sts increased.

Round 11: Same as Round 7.

Rounds 12-51: Repeat Rounds 4–11 five times more; 164 sts.

Round 52 (Increase Round): K to m, yo, sm, k1, sm, yo, k to end of round; 2 sts increased.

Round 53: Kw2 to m, sm, sl1 wyib, sm, kw2 to end of round.

Round 54 (Increase Round): Dropping extra wraps from kw2 in previous round, k to m, yo, sm, k1, sm, yo, k to end of round; 2 sts increased.

Round 55: P to m, sm, sl1 wyib, sm, p to end of round.

Rounds 56-59: Repeat Rounds 52–55 once more; 172 sts.

Round 60: Purl.

Round 61: Knit.

Rounds 62-73: Repeat Rounds 60 & 61 six times more.

Work Jeny's Surprisingly Stretchy Bind Off (see page 119).

FINISHING

Cut yarn; weave in ends. Block to measurements.

MAGIC

Like Mist, Magic features a striping pattern. But here, the striping produces a color fade pattern. It is designed to work with garter and reverse stockinette, and it does not result in too many ends to weave in. This color fade is also easy to remember and as a result, you may find yourself adding it to everything. I know I do!

FINISHED MEASUREMENTS

(After Blocking)

- Neck Opening: 26" (65 cm)
- Depth: 20" (50 cm)

SHAPE

- Triangle (Kerchief)

GAUGE

- 24 sts and 56 rows/rounds = 4" (10 cm) in garter stitch, with yarn held double

YARN

- Manos del Uruguay Fino Miniskeins, 70% merino extrafine/30% Tussah silk, fingering, 90 yds/98 m (20 g), 1 set in 11 Ophelia
- Color A–429 Storm Glass
- Color B–407 Velvet Pincushion
- Color C–408 Opal
- Color D–436 Porcelain
- Color E–414 Ivory Letter-Opener

NEEDLES

- US 5 (3.75 mm) circular needles in 24" (60 cm) and 32" (80 cm) lengths or size needed to obtain gauge

NOTIONS

- 4 stitch markers

Color Fade

2 rows/rounds in new color.

2 rows/rounds in old color.

4 rows/rounds in new color.

2 rows/rounds in old color.

Continue pattern in new color.

SETUP AND INCREASE

Using shorter needles and Color A held double, begin with a Stockinette Tab (page 32); 9 sts. As your cowlette grows, switch to longer needles.

Row 1 (Increase Row Setup, RS): K3, pm, m1l, k1, m1r, pm, k1, pm, m1l, k1, m1r, pm, k3; 13 sts.

Row 2 (and every WS row): P3, sm, k to m, sm, sl1 wyif, sm, k to m, sm, p3.

Row 3 (Increase Row): K3, sm, m1l, k to m, m1r, sm, k1, sm, m1l, k to m, m1r, sm, k3; 4 sts increased.

Rows 4–59: Repeat Rows 2 & 3 twenty-eight times more; 129 sts.

Row 60: Same as Row 2.

Rows 61–84: Using Color B held double as the new color, repeat Row 3 followed by Row 2 twelve times more while working Color Fade; 177 sts.

Row 85 (Increase Row): Work Row 3 once more, removing the first and last stitch marker, do not turn work; 181 sts.

JOIN IN THE ROUND

Using backward loop method, cast on 1 st, pm for BOR and join to work in the round; 182 sts.

Continue the body in the round, in garter stitch, by alternating knit and purl rounds.

Round 1 (and every purl round, RS): P to m, sm, sl1 wyib, sm, p to end of round.

Round 2 (Increase Round): K to m, m1r, sm, k1, sm, m1l, k to end of round; 2 sts increased.

Rounds 3–12: Continuing in Color B held double, repeat Rounds 1 & 2 five times more; 194 sts.

Rounds 13–22: Using Color C held double as the new color, repeat Rounds 1 & 2 five times more while working Color Fade; 204 sts.

Rounds 23–36: Continuing in Color C held double, repeat Rounds 1 & 2 seven times more; 218 sts.

Rounds 37–46: Using Color D held double as the new color, repeat Rounds 1 & 2 five times more while working Color Fade; 228 sts.

Rounds 47–56: Continuing in Color D held double, repeat Rounds 1 & 2 five times more; 238 sts.

Rounds 57–66: Using Color E held double as the new color, repeat Rounds 1 & 2 five times more while working Color Fade; 248 sts.

Using Color E held double, work a picot bind off as instructed on page 119, but repeat steps until 1 stitch remains on left needle. Bind off this last stitch. Cut the working yarn, leaving a 12-inch (30 cm) tail, and pull it through the live stitch.

FINISHING

Weave in ends. Block to measurements.

PERSEPHONE

Knit with 100 percent organic linen yarn and featuring a floral cluster stitch, Persephone is perfect for welcoming the spring season.

FINISHED MEASUREMENTS

(After Blocking)

- Neck Opening: 24" (60 cm)
- Depth: 24" (60 cm)

SHAPE

- Triangle (Kerchief)

GAUGE

- 22 sts and 42 rows = 4" (10 cm) in garter stitch

YARN

- Quince & Co. Sparrow, 100% organic linen, fingering, 164 yds/150 m (50 g), 1 skein each in Milkweed (Color A) and Moon (Color B)

NEEDLES

- US 3 (3.25 mm) circular needles in 16" (40 cm) and 24" (60 cm) lengths or size needed to obtain gauge

NOTIONS

- 4 stitch markers

SETUP AND INCREASE

Using shorter needles and Color A, begin with Increase Setup in Stockinette Stitch (page 31); 9 sts. As your cowlette grows, switch to longer needles.

Row 1 (Increase Row Setup, RS): K3, pm, yo, k1, yo, pm, k1, pm, yo, k1, yo, pm, k3; 13 sts.

Row 2 (WS): P3, sm, k to m, sm, k1, sm, k to m, sm, p3.

Row 3 (Increase Row): K3, sm, yo, k to m, yo, sm, k1, sm, yo, k to m, yo, sm, k3; 4 sts increased.

Row 4 (and every WS row): P3, sm, k to m, sm, k1, sm, k to m, sm, p3.

Rows 5-50: Repeat Rows 3 & 4 twenty-three times more; 109 sts.

Row 51 (Increase Row): Work Row 3 once more, removing the first and last stitch marker, do not turn work; 113 sts.

JOIN IN THE ROUND

Using backward loop method, cast on 2 sts, pm in the center of these cast-on stitches for BOR and join to work in the round; 115 sts.

Round 1 (RS): Purl, slipping markers.

Cut Color A. Switch to Color B.

Round 2 (Increase Round): K to m, yo, sm, k1, sm, yo, k to end of round; 2 sts increased.

Round 3: K to m, sm, p1, sm, k to end of round.

Rounds 4-57: Repeat Rounds 2 & 3 twenty-eight times more; 171 sts.

Cut Color B. Do not turn work.

FLORAL CLUSTER EDGING

We will now be working flat to avoid purling and to create neater clusters.

Row 1 (Increase Row, RS): Using Color A, k to m, yo, sm, k1, sm, yo, k to end; 2 sts increased.

Row 2 (WS): Knit, slipping markers.

Rows 3-8: Repeat Rows 1 & 2 three times more; 181 sts.

Row 9: Using Color B, [K1 wrapping yarn twice around the needle] to m, yo, sm, k1, sm, yo, [k1 wrapping yarn twice around the needle] to end; do not count sts.

Row 10: [Sl next 3 sts to right needle. Letting the second loop drop, place slipped sts back on left needle, (k1, p1, k1) into all 3 sts] to 1 st before m, k1, sm, k1, sm, k1, [sl next 3 sts to right needle; letting the second loop drop, place slipped sts back on left needle, (k1, p1, k1) into all 3 sts] to end. Cut Color B.

Rows 11-18: Using Color A, repeat Rows 1–8 once more; 189 sts.

Cut Color A.

With RS facing and using Color B, work Jeny's Surprisingly Stretchy Bind Off (page 119).

FINISHING

Cut yarn; weave in ends. Block to measurements.

Use mattress stitch to seam edge (page 122).

WINGS

Wings uses a marling technique, which is when you hold two different colors at the same time to create a new color, along with a gentle color fade that adds interest to an array of easy-to-remember texture stitches. This cowlette gets its name from the closely placed picots that resemble feathered wings.

FINISHED MEASUREMENTS
(After Blocking)

- Neck Opening: 19" (47.5 cm)
- Depth: 11" (27.5 cm)

SHAPE

- Half-Pi

GAUGE

- 20 sts and 28 rows/rounds = 4" (10 cm) in stockinette stitch, with yarn held double

YARN

- Manos del Uruguay Fino Miniskeins, 70% merino extrafine/30% Tussah silk, fingering, 90 yds/98 m (20 g), 1 set in 11 Lydia
- Color A–408 Crystal Goblet
- Color B–421 Havisham
- Color C–407 Velvet Pincushion
- Color D–429 Storm Glass
- Color E–416 Amethyst Earring

NEEDLES

- US 7 (4.5 mm) circular needles in 24" (60 cm) and 32" (80 cm) lengths or size needed to obtain gauge

NOTIONS

- 2 stitch markers

SETUP AND INCREASE

Using shorter needles and Color A held double, begin with Increase Setup in Garter Stitch (page 30); 9 sts. As your cowlette grows, switch to longer needles.

Row 1 (Increase Row Setup, RS): K3, pm, [yo, k1] 3 times, yo, pm, k3; 13 sts.

Row 2 (WS): K3, sm, p to m, sm, k3.

Row 3: Knit, slipping markers.

Row 4 (and every WS row): K3, sm, p to m, sm, k3.

Row 5 (Increase Row): K3, sm, [yo, k1] to m, yo, sm, k3; 21 sts.

Row 6: WS row.

Rows 7–10: Repeat Rows 3 & 4 twice more.

Row 11 (Increase Row): Same as Row 5; 37 sts.

Row 12: WS row.

Rows 13-20: Repeat Rows 3 & 4 four times more.

Row 21 (Increase Row): Same as Row 5; 69 sts.

Row 22: WS Row.

Cut 1 strand of Color A. Switch to remaining strand of Color A and 1 strand of Color B held together.

Rows 23 & 24: Knit, slipping markers.

Row 25: Knit, slipping markers.

Row 26: WS row.

Row 27: Knit, slipping markers.

Row 28: Knit, slipping markers.

Rows 29-44: Repeat Rows 25–28 four times more.

Cut Color A. Switch to Color B held double.

Row 45 (Increase Row): K3, sm, [k1, m1] to m, sm, k3; 132 sts.

Row 46: K3, sm, p to m, sm, k3.

Row 47: K3, sm, [k1, sl1 wyib] to m, sm, k3.

Row 48: K3, sm, [sl1 wyif, p1] to m, sm, k3.

Row 49: Knit, slipping markers.

Row 50: K3, sm, p to m, sm, k3.

Row 51: K3, sm, [sl1 wyib, k1] to m, sm, k3.

Row 52: K3, sm, [p1, sl1 wyif] to m, sm, k3.

Row 53: Knit, slipping markers.

Row 54: K3, sm, p to m, sm, k3.

Rows 55-62: Repeat Rows 47–54 once more.

Row 63: Knit, slipping markers.

Cut 1 strand of Color B. Switch to remaining strand of Color B and 1 strand of Color C held together.

Row 64: Knit, slipping markers.

Row 65: Knit, removing markers, do not turn work.

JOIN IN THE ROUND

Using backward loop method, cast on 2 sts, pm in the center of these cast-on stitches for BOR and join to work in the round; 134 sts.

Round 1 (RS): [K1, p1] to end of round.

Round 2: Knit.

Round 3: [K1, p1] to end of round.

Rounds 4 & 5: Repeat Rounds 2 & 3 once more.

Cut Color B. Switch to Color C held double.

Rounds 6-9: Repeat Rounds 2 & 3 twice more.

Round 10: Knit.

Round 11: Purl.

Rounds 12 & 13: Repeat Rounds 10 & 11 once more.

Round 14 (Increase Round): [K1, m1] to end of round; 268 sts.

Cut 1 strand of Color C. Switch to remaining strand of Color C and 1 strand of Color D held together.

Round 15: Purl.

Round 16: Knit.

Round 17: [P2tog] to end of round.

Round 18: [Kfb] to end of round.

Cut Color C. Switch to Color D held double.

Round 19: Knit.

Rounds 20-23: Repeat Rounds 16–19 once more. Do not change colors.

Round 24: Knit.

Cut 1 strand of Color D. Switch to remaining strand of Color D and 1 strand of Color E held together.

Rounds 25 & 26: Repeat Rounds 17 & 18 once more.

Cut Color D. Hold Color E double.

Round 27: Knit.

Work the following picot bind off to end of round: [Using a knitted cast on, cast on 2 stitches, bind off 4 stitches, slip stitch from right to left needle].

FINISHING

Cut yarn; weave in ends. Block to measurements.

PLEASE NOTE that this picot bind off is different from those that appear in other patterns in this book. These picots sit quite close together, creating a different effect.

GATHER

Gather was designed with utility in mind. Whether you are a Brothers Grimm character collecting firewood during a full moon or just running errands at the local grocery store, Gather is designed to keep the heat in and the cold out. Gather also features triangular shaping on the front and the back, even after your work is joined in the round.

FINISHED MEASUREMENTS

(After Blocking)

- Neck Opening: 20" (50 cm)
- Depth: 11½" (29 cm)

SHAPE

- Triangle (Poncho)

GAUGE

- 24 sts and 32 rows/rounds = 4" (10 cm) in stockinette stitch

YARN

- Rowan Felted Tweed, 50% wool/ 25% viscose/25% alpaca, DK, 191 yds/ 175 m (50 g), 1 ball in 196 Barn Red

NEEDLES

- US 6 (4 mm) circular needles in 24" (60 cm) and 32" (80 cm) lengths or size needed to obtain gauge

NOTIONS

- 4 stitch markers

SETUP AND INCREASE

Using shorter needles, begin with a Stockinette Tab (page 32); 9 sts. As your cowlette grows, switch to longer needles.

Row 1 (Increase Row Setup, RS): K2, [kfsb] twice, k1, [kfsb] twice, k2; 13 sts.

Row 2 (Marker Placement, WS): P3, pm, p3, pm, p1, pm, p3, pm, p3.

Row 3 (Increase Row): K3, sm, kfsb, k to 1 st before m, kfsb, sm, k1, sm, kfsb, k to 1 st before m, kfsb, sm, k3; 4 sts increased.

Row 4 (and every WS row): Purl, slipping markers.

Rows 5-52: Repeat Rows 3 & 4 twenty-four times more; 113 sts.

Row 53 (Increase Row): Work Row 3 once more, removing first and last markers, do not turn work; 117 sts.

JOIN IN THE ROUND

Place marker, then using backward loop method, cast on 1 st, pm for BOR and join to work in the round; 118 sts.

Round 1 (RS): Knit, slipping markers.

Round 2 (Increase Round): Kfsb, k to 1 st before m, kfsb, sm, k1, sm, kfsb, k to 1 st before m, kfsb, sm, k1; 4 sts increased.

Rounds 3-13: Repeat Rounds 1 & 2 five times more, then work Round 1 once more; 142 sts.

Round 14: P2, [k2, p2] to m, sm, k1, sm, p2, [k2, p2] to m, sm, k1.

Round 15 (Increase Round): Kfsb, p1, [k2, p2] to 4 sts before m, k2, p1, kfsb, sm, k1, sm, kfsb, p1, [k2, p2] to 4 sts before m, k2, p1, kfsb, sm, k1; 146 sts.

Round 16: K1, p2, [k2, p2] to 1 st before m, k1, sm, k1, sm, k1, p2 [k2, p2] to 1 st before m, k1, sm, k1.

Round 17 (Increase Round): Kfsb, p2, [k2, p2] to 1 st before m, kfsb, sm, k1, sm, kfsb, p2, [k2, p2] to 1 st before m, kfsb, sm, k1; 150 sts.

Round 18: K2, [p2, k2] to m, sm, k1, sm, k2, [p2, k2] to m, sm, k1.

Round 19 (Increase Round): Kfsb, k1, p2, [k2, p2] to 2 sts before m, k1, kfsb, sm, k1, sm, kfsb, k1, p2, [k2, p2] to 2 sts before m, k1, kfsb, sm, k1; 154 sts.

Round 20: P1, k2, [p2, k2] to 1 st before m, p1, sm, k1, sm, p1, k2, [p2, k2] to 1 st before m, p1, sm, k1.

Round 21 (Increase Round): Kfsb, k2, [p2, k2] to 1 st before m, kfsb, sm, k1, sm, kfsb, k2, [p2, k2] to 1 st before m, kfsb, sm, k1; 158 sts.

Turn work so that WS is facing.

Bind off using Jeny's Surprisingly Stretchy Bind Off (page 119).

NECK

With RS facing, pick up and knit 120 sts at neck, pm for BOR, and join to work in the round.

Round 1 (RS): [K2, p2] to end of round.

Rounds 2-9: Repeat Round 1 eight times more.

Turn work so that WS is facing.

Work Jeny's Surprisingly Stretchy Bind Off.

FINISHING

Cut yarn; weave in ends. Block to measurements.

TRAVELER

Another utility cowlette, Traveler can be worn under a jacket as an extra defense against the wind. Under layers, it can even look like a traditional dickey or a false turtleneck.

FINISHED MEASUREMENTS

(After Blocking)

- Neck Opening: 20" (50 cm)
- Depth: 14" (35 cm)

SHAPE

- Triangle (Poncho)

GAUGE

- 24 sts and 32 rows/rounds = 4" (10 cm) in stockinette stitch

YARN

- Rowan Felted Tweed, 50% wool/ 25% viscose/25% alpaca, DK, 191 yds/ 175 m (50 g), 1 ball in 175 Cinnamon

NEEDLES

- US 6 (4 mm) circular needles in 24" (60 cm) and 32" (80 cm) lengths

NOTIONS

- 4 stitch markers

SETUP AND INCREASE

Using shorter needles, begin with a Stockinette Tab (page 32); 9 sts. As your cowlette grows, switch to longer needles.

Row 1 (Increase Row Setup, RS): K2, [kfb] twice, k1, [kfb] twice, k2; 13 sts.

Row 2 (Marker Placement, WS): P3, pm, k3, pm, sl1 wyif, pm, k3, pm, p3.

Row 3 (Increase Row): K3, sm, kfb, k to 1 st before m, kfb, sm, k1, sm, kfb, k to 1 st before m, kfb, sm, k3; 4 sts increased.

Row 4 (and every WS row): P3, sm, k to m, sm, sl1 wyif, sm, k to m, sm, p3.

Rows 5-58: Repeat Rows 3 & 4 twenty-seven times more; 125 sts.

Row 59 (Increase Row): Work Row 3 once more, removing first and last marker, do not turn work; 129 sts.

JOIN IN THE ROUND

Using backward loop method, cast on 1 st, pm for BOR and join to work in the round; 130 sts.

Round 1 (RS): P to m, sm, sl1 wyib, sm, p to end.

Round 2 (Increase Round): K1, kfb, k to 1 st before m, kfb, sm, k1, sm, kfb, k to 1 st before m, kfb; 4 sts increased.

Rounds 3-17: Repeat Rounds 1 & 2 seven times more, then work Round 1 once more; 162 sts.

Turn work so that WS is facing.

Work Jeny's Surprisingly Stretchy Bind Off (page 119).

NECK

With RS facing, pick up and knit 124 sts at neck, pm for BOR, and join to work in the round.

Round 1 (RS): [K1, p1] to end of round.

Repeat Round 1 until neckband measures 4¼" (10.5 cm).

Turn work so that WS is facing.

Work Jeny's Surprisingly Stretchy Bind Off.

FINISHING

Cut yarn; weave in ends. Block to measurements.

TWILL

While designing Twill, I aimed to create an elegant accessory that resembled woven fabric. While I've always admired weaving and have wanted to try it, with two spinning wheels collecting dust in my closet, I can't justify another fun fiber hobby. So, I enjoy handwoven pieces from the sidelines, indulging in two-color seed stitch instead, which, coincidentally, is used in this cowlette.

FINISHED MEASUREMENTS

(After Blocking)

- Neck Opening: 19" (47.5 cm)
- Depth: 10" (25 cm)

SHAPE

- Half-Pi

GAUGE

- 28 sts and 40 rows/rounds = 4" (10 cm) in garter stitch

YARN

- Blue Sky Fibers Metalico, 50% baby alpaca/50% silk, sport, 147 yds/134 m (50 g), 1 skein each in 1617 Sterling (Color A) and 1612 Platinum (Color B)

NEEDLES

- US 5 (3.75 mm) circular needles in 24" (60 cm) and 32" (80 cm) lengths or size needed to obtain gauge

NOTIONS

- 2 stitch markers

SETUP AND INCREASE

Using shorter needles and Color A, begin with Increase Setup in Stockinette Stitch (page 31); 9 sts. As your cowlette grows, switch to longer needles.

Row 1 (Increase Row Setup, RS): K3, pm, [m1, k1] 3 times, m1, pm, k3; 13 sts.

Row 2 (WS): P3, sm, k to m, sm, p3.

Row 3: Knit, slipping markers.

Row 4 (and every WS row): P3, sm, k to m, sm, p3.

Row 5 (Increase Row): K3, sm, [m1, k1] to m, m1, sm, k3; 21 sts.

Row 6: WS row.

Rows 7–10: Repeat Rows 3 & 4 twice more.

Row 11 (Increase Row): Same as Row 5; 37 sts.

Row 12: WS row.

Rows 13–20: Repeat Rows 3 & 4 four times more.

Row 21 (Increase Row): Same as Row 5; 69 sts.

Row 22: WS Row.

Rows 23–38: Repeat Rows 3 & 4 eight times more.

Row 39 (Increase Row): Same as Row 5; 133 sts.

Row 40: WS Row.

Row 41: Knit, removing markers, do not turn work.

JOIN IN THE ROUND

Using backward loop method, cast on 1 st, pm for BOR and join to work in the round; 134 sts.

Round 1 (RS): Knit.

Rounds 2-15: Repeat Round 1 fourteen times more.

Round 16 (Increase Round): [M1, k1] to end of round; 268 sts.

Round 17: Using Color B, knit.

Round 18: Using Color A, [k1, p1] to end of round.

Round 19: Using Color B, knit.

Round 20: Using Color A, [p1, k1] to end of round.

Rounds 21-24: Repeat Rounds 17–20 once more.

Cut Color B.

Round 25: Using Color A, knit.

Turn work so that WS is facing.

Work Jeny's Surprisingly Stretchy Bind Off (page 119).

FINISHING

Cut yarn; weave in ends. Block to measurements.

GOLDENROD

Recently, while on a car ride up north, my ever-observant husband pointed out his new favorite fall foliage: goldenrod. You can spot these plants easily on the roadside as they are often the only spark of color left among the browning leaves. Goldenrod was named for these late bloomers and designed to add textural interest–and a pop of color–to your next outfit.

FINISHED MEASUREMENTS

(After Blocking)

- Neck Opening: 22" (55 cm)
- Depth: 12" (30 cm)

SHAPE

- Half-Pi

GAUGE

- 16 sts and 32 rows/rounds = 4" (10 cm) in garter stitch

YARN

- Katia Merino Tweed, 51% merino/ 43% acrylic/6% viscose, worsted, 85 yds/ 80 m (50 g), 2 balls in Mustard 318

NEEDLES

- US 9 (5.5 mm) circular needles in 24" (60 cm) and 32" (80 cm) lengths or size needed to obtain gauge

NOTIONS

- 2 stitch markers

SETUP AND INCREASE

Using shorter needles, begin with Increase Setup in Garter Stitch (page 30); 9 sts. As your cowlette grows, switch to longer needles.

Row 1 (Increase Row Setup, RS): K3, pm, [m1, k1] 3 times, pm, k3; 12 sts.

Row 2 (WS): K3, sm, p to m, sm, k3.

Row 3: Knit, slipping markers.

Row 4 (and every WS row): K3, sm, p to m, sm, k3.

Row 5 (Increase Row): K3, sm, [m1, k1] to m, sm, k3; 18 sts.

Row 6: WS row.

Rows 7-10: Repeat Rows 3 & 4 twice more.

Row 11 (Increase Row): Same as Row 5; 30 sts.

Row 12: WS row.

Rows 13 & 14: K3, sm, [k1, p1] to m, sm, k3.

Rows 15 & 16: K3, sm, [p1, k1] to m, sm, k3.

Rows 17-20: Repeat Rows 13–16 once more.

Row 21 (Increase Row): Same as Row 5; 54 sts.

Row 22: WS row.

Row 23 (Increase Row): K3, sm, p to m, m1, sm, k3; 55 sts.

Row 24: WS row.

Rows 25 & 26: Knit, slipping markers.

Row 27: K3, sm, k1, [p1, k1] to m, sm, k3.

Row 28: K3, sm, p1, [k1, p1] to m, sm, k3.

Rows 29-36: Repeat Rows 25–28 twice more.

Rows 37-38: Repeat Rows 25 & 26 once more.

Row 39 (Increase Row): Same as Row 5, removing markers, do not turn work; 104 sts.

JOIN IN THE ROUND

Using backward loop method, cast on 4 stitches, pm in the center of these cast-on stitches for BOR and join to work in the round; 108 sts.

Round 1 (RS): Knit.

Round 2: Purl.

Round 3: [K2, p2] to end of round.

Round 4: K1, [p2, k2] to last 3 sts, p2, k1.

Round 5: [P2, k2] to end of round.

Round 6: P1, [k2, p2] to last 3 sts, k2, p1.

Rounds 7-30: Repeat Rounds 3–6 six times more.

Round 31: Knit.

Turn work so that WS is facing.

Work Jeny's Surprisingly Stretchy Bind Off (page 119).

FINISHING

Cut yarn; weave in ends. Block to measurements.

BLOSSOM

When flowers start to bloom again, they appear as small buds, like the bobbles featured on this simplified Japanese lace motif. The simple and relaxing half-pi body opens up to an intuitive bobbled lace that is actually easier than it looks!

FINISHED MEASUREMENTS
(After Blocking)

- Neck Opening: 20" (50 cm)
- Depth: 9" (22.5 cm)

SHAPE

- Half-Pi

GAUGE

- 28 sts and 36 rows/rounds = 4" (10 cm) in stockinette stitch

YARN

- Quince & Co. Piper, 40% super kid mohair/60% South African superfine merino wool, lace, 305 yds/279 m (50 g), 1 skein in Avocet

NEEDLES

- US 6 (4 mm) circular needles in 24" (60 cm) and 32" (80 cm) lengths or size needed to obtain gauge

NOTIONS

- 21 stitch markers

Special Stitches

Make Bobble (mb): [yo, k1] 3 times into same stitch, turn, sl1, p5, turn, sl1, k5, turn, [p2tog] 3 times, turn, s2kp2.

SETUP AND INCREASE

Using shorter needles, begin with Increase Setup in Garter Stitch (page 30); 9 sts. As your cowlette grows, switch to longer needles.

Row 1 (Increase Row Setup, RS): K3, pm, [yo, k1] 3 times, yo, pm, k3; 13 sts.

Row 2 (WS): K3, sm, p to m, sm, k3.

Row 3: Knit, slipping markers.

Row 4 (and every WS row): K3, sm, p to m, sm, k3.

Row 5 (Increase Row): K3, sm, [yo, k1] to m, yo, sm, k3; 21 sts.

Row 6: WS row.

Rows 7-10: Repeat Rows 3 & 4 twice more.

Row 11 (Increase Row): Same as Row 5; 37 sts.

Row 12: WS row.

Rows 13-20: Repeat Rows 3 & 4 four times more.

Row 21 (Increase Row): Same as Row 5; 69 sts.

Row 22: WS Row.

Rows 23-38: Repeat Rows 3 & 4 eight times more.

Row 39 (Increase Row): Same as Row 5; 133 sts.

Row 40: WS Row.

Rows 41–44: Work Rows 3 & 4 twice more.

Row 45: Knit, removing markers, do not turn work.

JOIN IN THE ROUND

Using backward loop method, cast on 1 st, pm for BOR and join to work in the round; 134 sts.

Round 1 (RS): Knit.

Rounds 2-33: Repeat Round 1 thirty-two times more.

Round 34 (Increase Round): [Yo, k1] to end of round; 268 sts.

While working Round 35, place a marker every 13 stitches. This will not only make counting stitches easier but will also help you keep track of the following lace rows.

Round 35 (Increase Round): K1, [m1, k53] to last 2 sts, k2; 273 sts.

WORK BLOSSOM CHART

Work 12 rounds of Blossom Chart, repeating 13-stitch pattern 21 times across all stitches.

BLOSSOM CHART WRITTEN INSTRUCTIONS

Round 1: [Ssk, k1, yo, k1, yo, k6, k2tog, k1] to end of round.

Round 2: Knit.

Round 3: [Ssk, k2, yo, k1, yo, k5, k2tog, k1] to end of round.

Round 4: Knit.

Round 5: [Ssk, k3, yo, k1, yo, k4, k2tog, k1] to end of round.

Round 6: Knit.

Round 7: [Ssk, k1, mb, k2, yo, k1, yo, k3, k2tog, k1] to end of round.

BLOSSOM CHART

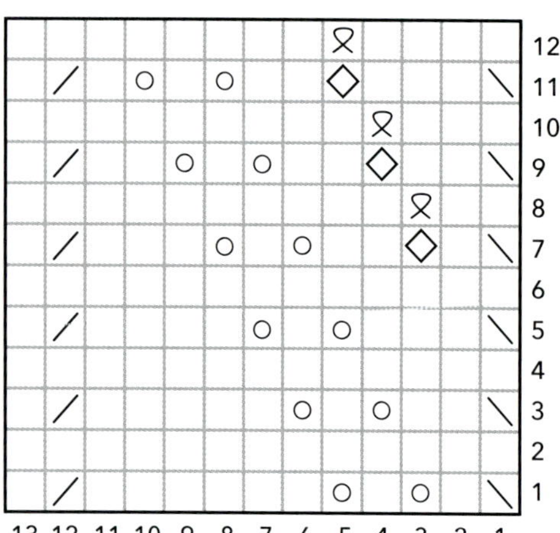

knit

mb (see Special Stitches, page 85)

ssk

k2tog

yo

k1 tbl

pattern repeat

Round 8: [K2, k1 tbl, k10] to end of round.

Round 9: [Ssk, k2, mb, k2, yo, k1, yo, k2, k2tog, k1] to end of round.

Round 10: [K3, k1 tbl, k9] to end of round.

Round 11: [Ssk, k3, mb, k2, yo, k1, yo, k1, k2tog, k1] to end of round.

Round 12: [K4, k1 tbl, k8] to end of round.

Turn work so that WS is facing.

Work Jeny's Surprisingly Stretchy Bind Off (page 119).

FINISHING

Cut yarn; weave in ends. Block to measurements.

ROYAL

Hailing from the Scottish Lowlands, houndstooth is another woven texture that I love. Is it historically regal? I think the jury is still out on that. Curiously (to me), in modern times, it is often used in business wear. But I think the check print has an aristocratic flair that I imagine a well-to-do antagonist would wear.

FINISHED MEASUREMENTS
(After Blocking)

- Neck Opening: 21" (52.5 cm)
- Depth: 16¼" (40.5 cm)

SHAPE

- Half-Pi

GAUGE

- 10 sts and 18 rows/rounds = 4" (10 cm) in stockinette stitch

YARN

- Katia Big Merino, 55% virgin wool/ 45% acrylic, bulky, 85 yds/80 m (100 g), 1 ball each in Light Beige 10 (Color A) and Black 2 (Color B)

NEEDLES

- US 11 (8 mm) circular needles in 24" (60 cm) and 32" (80 cm) lengths or size needed to obtain gauge

NOTIONS

- 2 stitch markers

SETUP AND INCREASE

Using shorter needles and Color A, begin with a Garter Tab (page 32); 9 sts. As your cowlette grows, switch to longer needles.

Row 1 (Increase Row Setup, RS): K3, pm, [m1, k1] 3 times, pm, k3; 12 sts.

Row 2 (WS): K3, sm, p to m, sm, k3.

Row 3: Knit, slipping markers.

Row 4 (and every WS row): K3, sm, p to m, sm, k3.

Row 5 (Increase Row): K3, sm, [m1, k1] to m, sm, k3; 18 sts.

Row 6: WS row.

Rows 7-10: Repeat Rows 3 & 4 twice more.

Row 11 (Increase Row): Same as Row 5; 30 sts.

Row 12: WS row.

Rows 13-20: Repeat Rows 3 & 4 four times more.

Row 21 (Increase Row): Same as Row 5; 54 sts.

Row 22: WS row.

Rows 23-26: Repeat Rows 3 & 4 twice more.

Row 27: Knit, removing markers, do not turn work.

JOIN IN THE ROUND

Using backward loop method, cast on 2 stitches, pm in the center of these cast-on stitches for BOR and join to work in the round; 56 sts.

Round 1 (RS): Knit.

Rounds 2-9: Repeat Round 1 eight times more.

Round 10 (Increase Round): [M1, k1] to end of round; 112 sts.

Round 11: Using Color B, knit.

Round 12: Using Color B, purl.

Rounds 13-24: Work Royal Chart 3 times.

ROYAL CHART

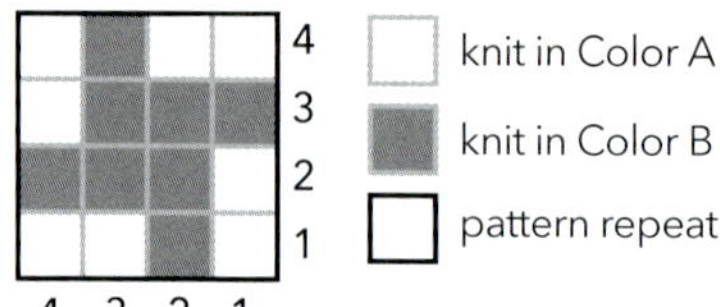

Cut Color A. Using Color B, work Jeny's Surprisingly Stretchy Bind Off (page 119).

FINISHING

Cut yarn; weave in ends. Block to measurements.

LI'L ONE

Li'l One is based on one of my earlier patterns, Baby Shawl. Baby Shawl was designed during the height of the 2020 lockdown when so many of my pattern testers didn't have a baby to model their finished piece. The next thing I knew, everyone was using their cats as models. As someone who accidentally found themself with three cats, this development got me thinking: What if we designed a cowlette with anyone or anything "li'l" in mind? Li'l One is different from the rest of the cowlettes in the book because it is not joined in the round; it has a button closure instead, so our li'l ones can easily take it off whenever they like.

FINISHED MEASUREMENTS
(After Blocking)

- Wingspan: 15½" (39 cm)
- Depth: 4½" (11.5 cm)

SHAPE

- Heart

GAUGE

- 24 sts and 40 rows = 4" (10 cm) in garter stitch

YARN

- Katia Merino Baby, 100% merino superwash, sport, 180 yds/165 m (50 g), 1 ball in Mint Green 86

NEEDLES

- US 3 (3.25 mm) 14" (35 cm) straight needles or circular needle 16" (40 cm) or longer or size needed to obtain gauge

NOTIONS

- 4 stitch markers, one ¾" (19 mm) button

SETUP AND INCREASES

Begin with Increase Setup in Stockinette Stitch (page 31); 9 sts.

Row 1 (Increase Row Setup, RS): K2, [kfb] twice, pm, k1, pm, [kfb] twice, k2; 13 sts.

Row 2 (Marker Placement, WS): K3, pm, k to m, sm, sl1 wyif, sm, k to 3 sts before end, pm, k3.

Row 3: K3, sm, [kfb] 3 times, sm, k1, sm, [kfb] 3 times, sm, k3; 19 sts.

Row 4: K3, sm, k to m, sm, sl1 wyif, sm, k to m, sm, k3.

Row 5 (Increase Row): K3, sm, [kfb] twice, k to 1 st before m, kfb, sm, k1, sm, kfb, k to 2 sts before m, [kfb] twice, sm, k3; 6 sts increased.

Row 6 (and every WS row): K3, sm, k to m, sm, sl1 wyif, sm, k to m, sm, k3.

Rows 7–36: Repeat Rows 5 & 6 fifteen times more; 115 sts.

Row 37 (Buttonhole Row, RS): K3, remove marker, yo, k to end, removing all markers.

Row 38: Knit.

Work Jeny's Surprisingly Stretchy Bind Off (page 119).

FINISHING

Cut yarn; weave in ends. Block to measurements.

Sew button onto end of cowlette opposite the buttonhole (see photo below). Weave in ends.

LI'L ONE, THE SEQUEL

This variation of Li'l One features garter stripes and an easy ruffle, and excludes the button. Some knitters like having a button; others are happy to fasten plain knitting through a yarnover. It's completely up to you!

FINISHED MEASUREMENTS

(After Blocking)

- Wingspan: 15½" (39 cm)
- Depth: 4½" (11.5 cm)

SHAPE

- Heart

GAUGE

- 24 sts and 40 rows = 4" (10 cm) in garter stitch

YARN

- Katia Merino Baby, 100% merino superwash, sport, 180 yds/165 m (50 g), 1 ball each in Light Gray 70 (Color A) and White 1 (Color B)

NEEDLES

- US 3 (3.25 mm) 14" (35 cm) straight needles or circular needle 16" (40 cm) or longer or size needed to obtain gauge

NOTIONS

- 4 stitch markers

SETUP AND INCREASE

Using Color A, begin with Increase Setup in Garter Stitch (page 30); 9 sts.

Row 1 (WS): K2, [kfb] twice, pm, k1, pm, [kfb] twice, k2; 13 sts.

Row 2 (Marker Placement, RS): Using Color B, k3, pm, k to m, sm, k1, sm, k to 3 sts before end, pm, k3.

Row 3 (and every WS row): Knit, slipping markers.

Row 4: K3, sm, [kfb] 3 times, sm, k1, sm, [kfb] 3 times, sm, k3; 19 sts.

Row 5: WS Row.

Row 6 (Increase Row): Using Color A, k2, sm, [kfb] twice, sm, k to 1 st before m, kfb, sm, k1, sm, kfb, k to 2 sts before m, [kfb] twice, sm, k3; 6 sts increased.

Row 7: Knit, slipping markers.

Rows 8-37: Repeat Rows 6 & 7 fifteen times more, continuing color pattern that alternates between Color A and B every fourth row; 115 sts, ending with Color B.

Cut Color B.

Row 38 (Increase Row, RS): Using Color A, [yo, k1] to end.

Rows 39-41: Using Color A, knit.

Work Jeny's Surprisingly Stretchy Bind Off (page 119).

FINISHING

Cut yarn; weave in ends. Block to measurements.

JUNE

Perfect for warmer weather, June looks great worn askew, allowing the dramatic heart shape to shine. The two-color feather-and-fan lace resembles summer's blooming flowers.

FINISHED MEASUREMENTS

(After Blocking)

- Neck Opening: 24" (60 cm)
- Depth: 8½" (21.5 cm)

SHAPE

- Heart

GAUGE

- 36 sts and 44 rows/rounds = 4" (10 cm) in stockinette stitch

YARN

- Madelinetosh Tosh Merino Light, 100% superwash merino wool, fingering, 420 yds/384 m (105 g), 1 skein each in Copper Pink/Solid (Color A) and Mars Rover (Color B)

NEEDLES

- US 6 (4 mm) circular needle in 24" (60 cm) length or size needed to obtain gauge

NOTIONS

- 4 stitch markers

SETUP AND INCREASE

Using Color A, begin with Increase Setup in Garter Stitch (page 30); 9 sts.

Row 1 (Increase Row Setup, RS): K3, pm, yo, k1, yo, pm, k1, pm, yo, k1, yo, pm, k3; 13 sts.

Row 2 (WS): K3, sm, p to m, sm, p1, sm, p to m, sm, k3.

Row 3 (Increase Row): K3, sm, yo, k1, yo, k to m, yo, sm, k1, sm, yo, k to 1 st before m, yo, k1, yo, sm, k3; 6 sts increased.

Row 4 (and every WS Row): K3, sm, p to m, sm, sl1 wyif, sm, p to m, sm, k3.

Rows 5-62: Repeat Rows 3 & 4 twenty-nine times more; 193 sts.

Row 63: Knit, removing markers, do not turn work.

JOIN IN THE ROUND

Using backward loop method, cast on 5 sts, pm for BOR and join to work in the round; 198 sts.

TWO-COLOR FEATHER-AND-FAN MOTIF

Work the Two-Color Feather-and-Fan motif:

Round 1 (RS): Using Color A, knit.

Round 2: Using Color A, purl.

Rounds 3 & 4: Using Color B, knit.

Round 5: *Using Color B, [k2tog] 3 times, [yo, k1] 6 times, [k2tog] 3 times; repeat from * to end of round.

Round 6: Using Color B, knit.

Round 7: Using Color A, knit.

Rounds 8-21: Work Rounds 1–7 twice more.

Turn work so that WS is facing.

Work Jeny's Surprisingly Stretchy Bind Off (page 119).

FINISHING

Cut yarn; weave in ends. Block to measurements.

MOONSTONE

The ruffles on this cowlette, along with the hand-dyed nature of the yarn, give Moonstone the look of an old traveler's cloak gliding along a path in the moonlight.

FINISHED MEASUREMENTS
(After Blocking)
- Neck Opening: 21" (52.5 cm)
- Depth: 12" (30 cm)

SHAPE
- Half-Pi

GAUGE
- 30 sts and 38 rows/rounds = 4" (10 cm) in stockinette stitch

YARN
- Manos del Uruguay Alegria, 75% superwash merino wool/25% polyamide, fingering, 445 yds/425 m (100 g), 1 skein in A7090 Nobuk

NEEDLES
- US 6 (4 mm) circular needles in 24" (60 cm) and 32" (80 cm) lengths or size needed to obtain gauge

NOTIONS
- 2 stitch markers

SETUP AND INCREASE

Using shorter needles, begin with Increase Setup in Garter Stitch (page 30); 9 sts. As your cowlette grows, switch to longer needles.

Row 1 (Increase Row Setup, RS): K3, pm, [kfsb] 3 times, pm, k3; 12 sts.

Row 2 (WS): K3, sm, p to m, sm, k3.

Row 3: Knit, slipping markers.

Row 4 (and every WS Row): K3, sm, p to m, sm, k3.

Row 5 (Increase Row): K3, sm, [ksfb] to m, sm, k3; 18 sts.

Row 6: WS row.

Rows 7-10: Repeat Rows 3 & 4 twice more.

Row 11 (Increase Row): Same as Row 5; 30 sts.

Row 12: WS row.

Rows 13-20: Repeat Rows 3 & 4 four times more.

Row 21 (Increase Row): Same as Row 5; 54 sts.

Row 22: WS Row.

Rows 23-38: Repeat Rows 3 & 4 eight times more.

Row 39 (Increase Row): Same as Row 5; 102 sts.

Row 40: WS Row.

Rows 41-52: Repeat Rows 3 & 4 six times more.

Row 53: Knit, removing markers, do not turn work.

JOIN IN THE ROUND

Using backward loop method, cast on 4 stitches, pm in the center of these stitches for BOR and join to work in the round; 106 sts.

RUFFLED GATHER STITCH MOTIF

Work the Ruffled Gather Stitch motif:

Round 1 (RS): Knit.

Round 2 (Increase Round): [Kfsb] to end of round; 212 sts.

Rounds 3-7: Knit.

Round 8 (Decrease Round): [K2tog] to end of round; 106 sts.

Round 9 (Increase Round): Same as Round 2; 212 sts.

Rounds 10-14: Knit.

Round 15 (Decrease Round): Same as Round 8; 106 sts.

Round 16 (Increase Round): [K1, yo] to end of round; 212 sts.

Rounds 17 & 18: Knit.

Round 19 (Increase Round): Same as Round 16; 424 sts.

Rounds 20-25: Knit.

Round 26: Purl.

Round 27: Knit.

Round 28: Purl.

Work Jeny's Surprisingly Stretchy Bind Off (page 119).

FINISHING

Cut yarn; weave in ends. Block to measurements.

BLOCKING TIP

Earlier, I talked about how much I love ironing as a blocking method for cowlettes, but Moonstone is one that I recommend soaking and draping across a hanger to dry. There are so many fabric changes happening in Moonstone—plain stockinette, gathers, and ruffles. A good soak will help the stitches relax effectively, and you won't accidentally steam the gathers into pleats.

BETROTHED

Delicate and ethereal, Betrothed is reminiscent of a Russian Orenburg shawl, which is a large shawl that is knit at such a fine gauge that it can be pulled through a wedding ring. This type of shawl is mostly known to English-speaking knitters as a Wedding Ring Shawl. Though Betrothed is smaller in size and worked at a larger gauge than a traditional Orenburg shawl, it uses a simple lace motif that is accessible for modern knitters.

FINISHED MEASUREMENTS
(After Blocking)

- Neck Opening: 22" (55 cm)
- Depth: 9½" (24 cm)

SHAPE

- Heart

GAUGE

- 32 sts and 40 rows/rounds = 4" (10 cm) in stockinette stitch

YARN

- Quince & Co. Piper, 40% super kid mohair/60% South African superfine merino, lace, 305 yds/279 m (50 g), 1 skein in Blanco

NEEDLES

- US 5 (3.75 mm) circular needles in 24" (60 cm) and 32" (80 cm) lengths or size needed to obtain gauge

NOTIONS

- 4 stitch markers

SETUP AND INCREASE

Using shorter needles and Color A, begin with Increase Setup in Garter Stitch (page 30); 9 sts. As your cowlette grows, switch to longer needles.

Row 1 (Increase Setup Row, RS): K3, pm, yo, k1, yo, pm, k1, pm, yo, k1, yo, pm, k3; 13 sts.

Row 2 (WS): K3, sm, p to m, sm, p1, sm, p to m, sm, k3.

Row 3 (Increase Row): K3, sm, yo, k1, yo, k to m, yo, sm, k1, sm, yo, k to 1 st before m, yo, k1, yo, sm, k3; 6 sts increased.

Row 4 (and every WS Row): K3, sm, p to m, sm, p1, sm, p to m, sm, k3.

Rows 5-58: Repeat Rows 3 & 4 twenty-seven times more; 181 sts.

Row 59 (Increase Row): Work Row 3 once more, removing the first and last stitch marker, do not turn work; 187 sts.

JOIN IN THE ROUND

Using backward loop method, cast on 1 stitch, place marker for BOR and join to work in the round; 188 sts.

Round 1 (Increase Round, RS): K to m, yo, sm, k1, sm, yo, k to end of round; 2 sts increased.

Round 2: Knit.

Rounds 3 & 4: Repeat Rounds 1 & 2 once more; 192 sts. Remove BOR marker.

BETROTHED LACE EDGING

Turn work to WS. Using cable method, cast on 7 stitches to left needle, do not turn work.

We will now be working perpendicular to our knitting to create a sideways lace edge. Every WS row will end with a p2tog, which is worked with 1 Betrothed Lace stitch and 1 stitch from the cowlette body.

Setup Row (WS): K6, p2tog, turn.

Using the chart or written instructions, work the 4 rows of Betrothed Lace 95 times, then repeat Rows 1 & 2 of the lace once more, until all body stitches are consumed.

BETROTHED LACE CHART WRITTEN INSTRUCTIONS

Row 1 (RS): Sl1 wyib, k1, k2tog, yo, k2, [yo] twice, k1; 9 sts.

Row 2 (WS): K1, k1 into first yo, k1 tbl into 2nd yo, k2tog, yo, k3, p2tog, turn work.

Row 3: Sl1 wyib, k1, k2tog, yo, k5.

Row 4: Bind off 2 sts, k2tog, yo, k3, p2tog, turn work; 7 sts.

Bind off in pattern.

FINISHING

Block to measurements. Use mattress stitch to seam the cast on to the bind off (page 122).

Cut yarn; weave in ends.

BETROTHED LACE CHART

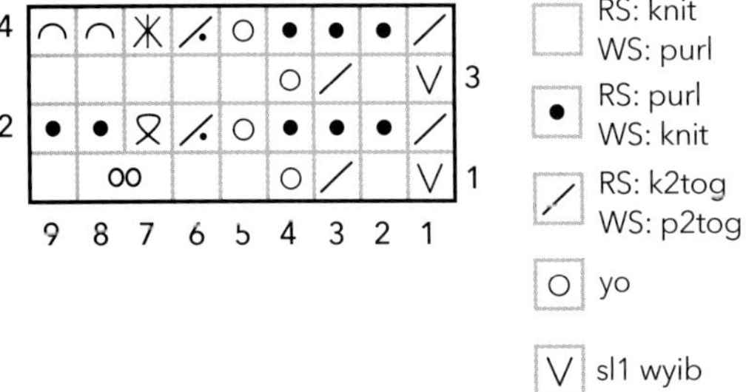

RS: p2tog
WS: k2tog

k1 tbl

bind off

yarnover twice

Indicates stitch remaining on right needle after completing a bind off

pattern repeat

GOLDSPUN

Forever ethereal, Goldspun was designed with faeries and elves in mind. This grand cowlette looks like something out of a favorite fantasy book, and it pairs nicely with formal attire in real life. Goldspun differs from other cowlettes because it is larger and resembles a capelet. You can adjust the depth to your liking using the suggested depth measurements. Just pick a size based on how long you would like your cowlette to drape across your torso.

SIZES

- 1 [2, 3, 4]

FINISHED MEASUREMENTS

(After Blocking)

- Neck Opening (all sizes): 21" (52.5 cm)
- Depth (from join in back): 10 [12, 14½, 16½]" (25 [30, 36.5, 41.5] cm)

SHAPE

- Half-Pi

GAUGE

- 36 sts and 44 rows/rounds = 4" (10 cm) in stockinette stitch

YARN

- Blue Sky Fibers Metalico, 50% alpaca/ 50% silk, sport, 147 yds/134 m (50 g), 2 [2, 3, 4] skeins in 1632 Gold Topaz, approximately 294 [294, 441, 588] yds/ 269 [269, 403, 538] m (100 [100, 150, 200] g

NEEDLES

- US 6 (4 mm) circular needles in 24" (60 cm) and 32" (80 cm) lengths or size needed to obtain gauge

NOTIONS

- 2 stitch markers

SETUP AND INCREASE

Using shorter needles, begin with a Garter Tab (page 32); 9 sts. As your cowlette grows, switch to longer needles.

Row 1 (Increase Row Setup, RS): K3, pm, [kfsb] 3 times, pm, k3; 12 sts.

Row 2 (WS): K3, sm, p to m, sm, k3.

Row 3: Knit, slipping markers.

Row 4 (and every WS row): K3, sm, p to m, sm, k3.

Row 5 (Increase Row): K3, sm, [kfsb] to m, sm, k3; 18 sts.

Row 6: WS row.

Rows 7-10: Repeat Rows 3 & 4 twice more.

Row 11 (Increase Row): Same as Row 5; 30 sts.

Row 12: WS row.

Rows 13-20: Repeat Rows 3 & 4 four times more.

Row 21 (Increase Row): Same as Row 5; 54 sts.

Row 22: WS row.

Rows 23-38: Repeat Rows 3 & 4 eight times more.

Row 39 (Increase Row): Same as Row 5; 102 sts.

Row 40: WS row.

Rows 41-50: Repeat Rows 3 & 4 five times more.

Row 51: Knit, removing markers, do not turn work.

JOIN IN THE ROUND

Using backward loop method, cast on 2 stitches, pm in the center of these stitches for BOR and join to work in the round; 104 sts.

Round 1 (RS): Knit.

Rounds 2-20: Repeat Round 1 nineteen times more.

Round 21 (Increase Round): [Kfsb] to end of round; 208 sts.

Continue in stockinette until work measures 9 [11, 13½, 15½]" (22.5 [27.5, 34, 39] cm) from join.

LACE EDGE

Work the following lace edge:

Round 1: [Yo, k2tog] to end of round.

Round 2: [K2tog, yo] to end of round.

Rounds 3 & 4: Knit.

Work a picot bind off (page 119) to last stitch; bind off last stitch.

FINISHING

Cut yarn; weave in ends. Block to measurements.

JANUARY

The foil of June, January holds the yarn double, creating a new fabric and color while still using the same yarn. In fact, if you use the recommended yarn, you will have enough yarn to knit January and June, and I highly recommend knitting both as a set. I just think they go so well together!

FINISHED MEASUREMENTS
(After Blocking)

- Neck Opening: 19" (47.5 cm)
- Depth: 9¼" (23 cm)

SHAPE

- Triangle (Kerchief)

GAUGE

- 20 sts and 40 rows/rounds = 4" (10 cm) in garter stitch with yarn held double

YARN

- Madelinetosh Tosh Merino Light, 100% superwash merino wool, fingering, 420 yds/384 m (115 g), 1 skein each in Mars Rover (Color A) and Copper Pink/ Solid (Color B)

NEEDLES

- US 7 (4.5 mm) circular needles in 24" (60 cm) and 32" (80 cm) lengths or size needed to obtain gauge

NOTIONS

- 4 stitch markers

SETUP AND INCREASE

Using shorter needles and 1 strand of Color A and 1 strand of Color B held together, begin with a Stockinette Tab (page 32); 9 sts. As your cowlette grows, switch to longer needles.

Row 1 (Increase Row Setup, RS): K3, pm, yo, k1, yo, pm, k1, pm, yo, k1, yo, pm, k3; 13 sts.

Row 2 (WS): P3, sm, k to m, sm, sl1 wyif, sm, k to m, sm, p3.

Row 3 (Increase Row): K3, sm, yo, k to m, yo, sm, k1, sm, yo, k to m, yo, sm, k3; 4 sts increased.

Row 4 (and every WS row): P3, sm, k to m, sm, sl1 wyif, sm, k to m, sm, p3.

Rows 5-46: Repeat Rows 3 & 4 twenty-one times more; 101 sts.

Row 47 (Increase Row): Same as Row 3; 105 sts.

Row 48: Work Row 4 once more, removing first and last markers, do not turn work.

JOIN IN THE ROUND

Using backward loop method, cast on 2 sts, pm for BOR, cast on 1 stitch and join to work in the round; 108 sts.

Next Round (RS): P to m, sm, sl1 wyib, sm, p to end of round.

TWO-COLOR FEATHER-AND-FAN MOTIF

Work the following Two-Color Feather-and-Fan motif:

Round 1: Using Color A held double, knit.

Round 2: Using Color A held double, purl.

Rounds 3 & 4: Using Color B held double, knit.

Round 5: *Using Color B held double, [k2tog] 3 times, [yo, k1] 6 times, [k2tog] 3 times; repeat from * to end of round.

Round 6: Using Color B held double, knit.

Rounds 7-26: Work Rounds 1–6 three times more, then work Rounds 1 & 2 once more.

Cut Color A.

Using Color B, work a picot bind off (page 119).

FINISHING

Cut yarn; weave in ends. Block to measurements.

Design Your Own Cowlette

Once you have knitted a cowlette (or two or three), I highly encourage you to take a leap of faith and design your own. I have taken all of the guesswork out of the process by creating a few tools to guide you on your design adventure:

- The Cowlette Knitter's Worksheet (page 112) provides you with a template for recording essential information about your design.
- Steps for Designing a Cowlette (page 113) walks you through the five crucial steps of cowlette construction (setup, shaping, joining in the round, continuing in the round to desired length, and finishing).
- The Cowlette Shaping Cheat Sheet (page 114) is a step-by-step reference for working your stitch increase of choice, once you have decided on the shape of your cowlette.

To get started, first choose your yarn and needles, and knit a swatch. Then use the Cowlette Knitter's Worksheet to record your project name, yarn, needles, gauge, shape, desired neck-opening circumference, and rows needed. Next, use the Steps for Designing a Cowlette to help you fill out setup type, increase type, and your row counts. While you work, use the Cowlette Shaping Cheat Sheet as needed to keep your knitting on track.

Ready? Let's go!

COWLETTE KNITTER'S WORKSHEET

Use this customizable template to design your own cowlette. Let any of the patterns in this book serve as inspiration for creating a unique design that fits your individual needs.

YOUR PROJECT NAME:

Yarn:

Needles:

Gauge (rows per inch [cm]/stitch used):

Cowlette shape:

Desired neck-opening circumference:

Desired depth:

Rows needed for circumference *(see page 34)**:*

Setup type:

Increase type:

Step 2 stitch and row count:

Step 3 stitch and row count:

Step 4 stitch and row count:

Finished neck-opening circumference:

Finished depth:

STEPS FOR DESIGNING A COWLETTE

STEP 1: SETUP

Using a setup (see page 30), increase to 9 sts.

STEP 2: SHAPING

Choose a shape (page 26) and shaping increase (page 35), and follow the pattern increase steps on the Cowlette Shaping Cheat Sheet (page 114) until you reach the desired neck-opening circumference (page 34).

STEP 3: JOINING IN THE ROUND

On the next right-side row, work in pattern until end of row, removing the first and last stitch markers, do not turn work. Using the backward loop method, cast on 1 stitch (or more; see Author's Note below), pm for BOR and join to work in the round.

STEP 4: CONTINUING IN THE ROUND

Continue the shaping increases in pattern until the cowlette reaches your desired length.

Important note: When working a triangular cowlette in the kerchief shape, you will only work the center increases to shape just the front. For a triangular poncho shape, continue working at the same increase rate as before joining, shaping at both front and back.

STEP 5: FINISHING

Work your desired bind off. Weave in ends, closing any gaps. Wash and block your work as desired.

Author's Note: In some of my patterns, I cast on multiple stitches as part of joining in the round. Typically, this is to adjust my stitch counts for future motifs. When casting on multiple stitches, I place my beginning-of-the-round marker in the center of my cast-on stitches.

COWLETTE SHAPING CHEAT SHEET

TRIANGLE COWLETTES

Follow the step-by-step instructions using your desired type of increase.

KFB OR KFSB INCREASES

Once you have 9 setup stitches on the needle, work Rows 1 & 2:

Row 1 (Increase Row Setup, RS): Work 2 sts in pattern, [kfb or kfsb] twice, work 1 st, [kfb or kfsb twice], work to end; 13 sts.

Row 2 (Marker Placement, WS): Work 3 sts in pattern, pm, work 3 sts, pm, work 1 st, pm, work 3 sts, pm, work to end.

Row 3 (Increase Row, RS): Work in pattern to marker, sm, kfb or kfsb, work to 1 st before m, kfb or kfsb, sm, work 1 st, sm, kfb or kfsb, work to m, kfb or kfsb, work to end; 4 sts increased.

Row 4 (WS): Work in pattern, slipping markers.

Continue the pattern by repeating Rows 3 & 4 until your work reaches your desired cowlette circumference. Then proceed to Step 3: Joining in the Round on page 113.

YARNOVER INCREASES

Once you have 9 setup stitches on the needle, work Rows 1 & 2:

Row 1 (Increase Row Setup, RS): Work 3 sts in pattern, pm, yo, work 1 st, yo, pm, work 1 st, pm, yo, work 1 st, yo, pm, work to end; 13 sts.

Row 2 (WS): Work in pattern, slipping markers.

Row 3 (Increase Row, RS): Work in pattern to marker, sm, yo, work to m, yo, sm, work 1 st, sm, yo, work to end, slipping the final marker; 4 sts increased.

Row 4 (WS): Work in pattern, slipping markers.

Continue the pattern by repeating Rows 3 & 4 until your work reaches your desired cowlette circumference. Then proceed to Step 3: Joining in the Round on page 113.

M1R AND M1L INCREASES

Once you have 9 setup stitches on the needle, work Rows 1 & 2:

Row 1 (Increase Row Setup, RS): Work 3 sts in pattern, pm, m1l, work 1 st, m1r, pm, work 1 st, pm, m1l, work 1 st, m1r, pm, work to end; 13 sts.

Row 2 (WS): Work in pattern, slipping markers.

Row 3 (Increase Row, RS): Work 3 sts in pattern, sm, m1l, work to m, m1r, sm, work 1 st, sm, m1l, work to m, m1r, sm, work to end; 4 sts increased.

Row 4 (WS): Work in pattern, slipping markers.

Continue the pattern by repeating Rows 3 & 4 until your work reaches your desired cowlette circumference. Then proceed to Step 3: Join in the Round on page 113.

HALF-PI COWLETTES

Follow the step-by-step instructions using your desired type of increase.

KFB OR KFSB INCREASES

Once you have your 9 setup stitches on the needle, work Rows 1 & 2:

Row 1 (Increase Row Setup, RS): Work 3 sts in pattern, pm, [kfb or kfsb] to last 3 sts, pm, work to end; 12 sts.

Row 2 (WS): Work in pattern, slipping markers.

Rows 3 & 4: Work in pattern, slipping markers.

Row 5 (Increase Row, RS): Work 3 sts in pattern, sm, [kfb or kfsb] to last 3 sts, sm, work 3 sts; stitch count between markers will double.

Row 6 (WS): Work in pattern, slipping markers.

Rows 7–10: Work in pattern, slipping markers.

Continue the pattern by repeating an Increase Row and then doubling the number of plain knitting rows after each Increase Row (see Shaping Increases, page 35).

YARNOVER INCREASES

When working yarnover increases in half-pi cowlettes, add an additional yarnover at the end of the row, right before the edge stitches. This extra yarnover is only for symmetry. Although it adds an extra stitch, this does not affect the overall shape of your cowlette because you are still increasing at the correct intervals.

Once you have 9 setup stitches on the needle, work Rows 1 & 2:

Row 1 (Increase Row Setup, RS): Work 3 sts in pattern, pm, [yo, work 1 st] to last 3 sts, yo, pm, work to end; 13 sts.

Row 2: Work in pattern, slipping markers.

Rows 3 & 4: Work in pattern, slipping markers.

Row 5 (Increase Row): Work in pattern to marker, sm, [yo, work 1 st] to m, yo, sm, work to end; stitch count between markers will double + 1.

Row 6: Work in pattern, slipping markers.

Rows 7–10: Work in pattern, slipping markers.

Continue the pattern by repeating an Increase Row and then doubling the number of plain knitting rows after each Increase Row (see Shaping Increases, page 35).

M1R AND M1L INCREASES

When working a half-pi cowlette, you need to choose one of these increases, either m1r or m1l, and then use that increase for the entirety of the cowlette. That's why in the following instructions, I use m1 to signify when it is your choice. Just choose the increase that's easiest for you to execute and stick to that for the entire duration of your cowlette knitting. (My students and I find the m1l to be slightly easier to execute than the m1r.)

Once you have 9 setup stitches on the needle, work Rows 1 & 2:

Row 1 (Increase Row Setup, RS): Work 3 sts in pattern, pm, [m1, work 1 st] to last 3 sts, pm, work to end; 12 sts.

CONTINUED ON PAGE 116

Row 2: Work in pattern, slipping markers.

Rows 3 & 4: Work in pattern, slipping markers.

Row 5 (Increase Row): Work in pattern to marker, sm, [m1, work 1] to m, m1, sm, work to end; stitch count between markers will double + 1.

Row 6: Work in pattern, slipping markers.

Rows 7–10: Work in pattern, slipping markers.

Continue the pattern by repeating an Increase Row and then doubling the number of plain knitting rows after each Increase Row (see Shaping Increases, page 35).

GLOSSARY OF TECHNIQUES

Cast Ons

LONG-TAIL CAST ON

SETUP

1. Use one needle and a single strand of yarn. Pull out a length of yarn that is at least 6 inches (15 cm). Make a slip knot here and place it on the needle. Hold the needle in your right hand with your index finger on the slip knot.
2. With your left hand, wrap the long tail around your thumb counterclockwise and the working yarn around your index finger clockwise, as shown. The long tail should be closest to you (in front of the needle) while the working yarn is farther from you (behind the needle). Your thumb and index finger should form a "V".
3. Secure both tails of your yarn with the rest of your fingers. You will keep these two strands secured in your left hand for the rest of the cast on.

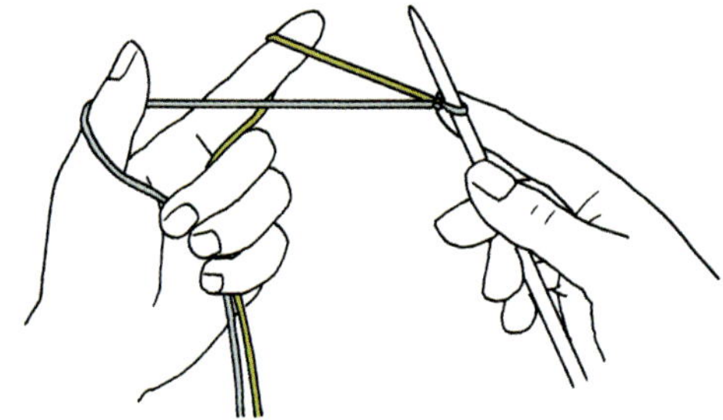

WORKING

1. Insert the needle from below, into the loop around your thumb.

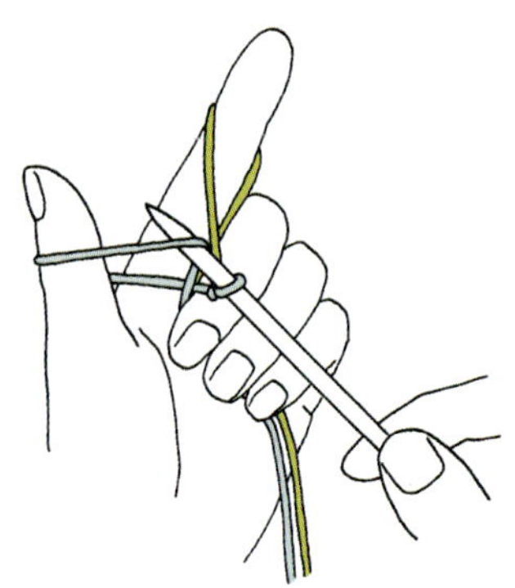

2. Bring the needle in front of, then behind, the strand on your index finger.

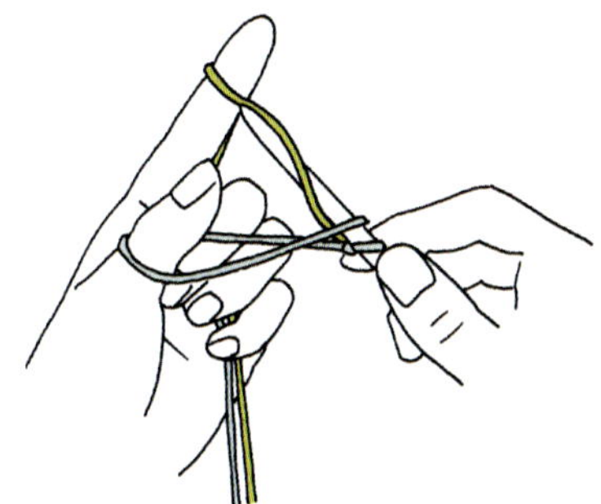

3. Bring the needle through the thumb loop.

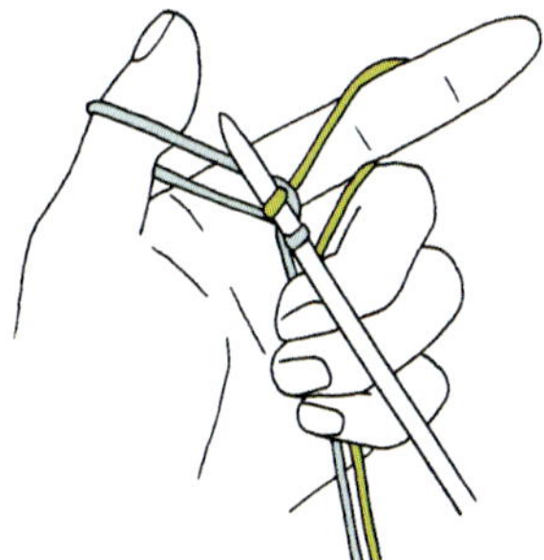

4. Slip the loop off your thumb.
5. Place your thumb behind the long tail and pull it gently against the tail to tighten the loop. One stitch has been cast on. To keep the edge of your knitting stretchy, make sure to leave a little room between the stitches on the needle. In other words, don't snug them together too closely.

Repeat steps 1–5 until you have the desired number of cast-on stitches, being sure to include the original slip knot as the first stitch in your count.

LONG-TAIL PROVISIONAL CAST ON

SETUP

1. Use one needle, a single strand of yarn, and a single strand of scrap yarn. For each strand, pull out a length of yarn that is at least 6 inches (15 cm). Using both strands, make a slip knot here and place it on the needle. Hold the needle in your right hand with your index finger on the slip knot.
2. With your left hand, wrap the scrap yarn around your thumb counterclockwise and the working yarn around your index finger clockwise, as shown. The scrap yarn should be closest to you (in front of the needle) while the working yarn is farther from you (behind the needle). Your thumb and index finger should form a "V".
3. Secure both tails of your yarn with the rest of your fingers. You will keep these two strands secured in your left hand for the rest of the cast on.

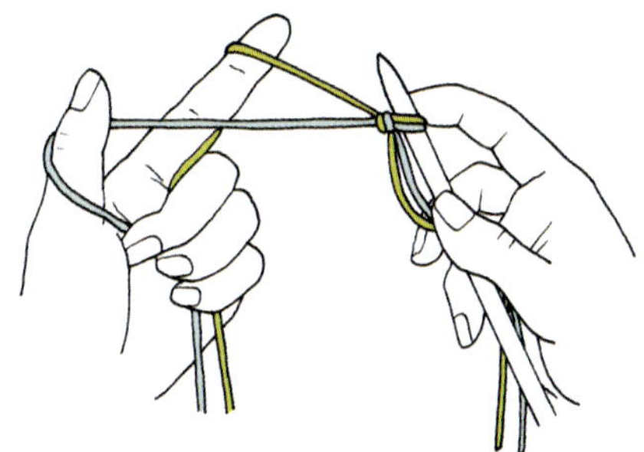

WORKING

1. Insert the needle from below, into the loop of scrap yarn around your thumb.

CONTINUED ON PAGE 118

2. Bring the needle in front of, then behind, the strand of working yarn on your index finger.

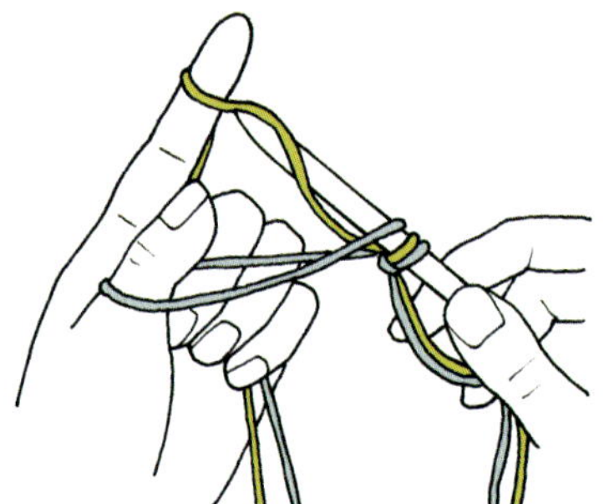

3. Bring the needle through the thumb loop.

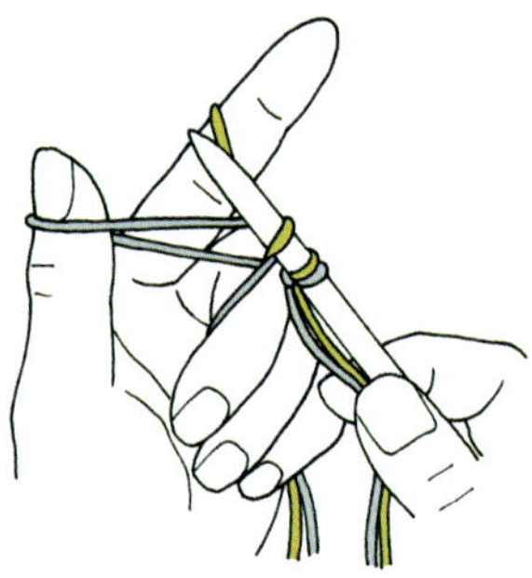

4. Slip the loop off your thumb.

5. Place your thumb behind the long tail and pull it gently against the tail to tighten the loop. To keep the edge of your knitting stretchy, make sure to leave a little room between the stitches on the needle. In other words, don't snug them together too closely.

Repeat steps 1–5 until you have the desired number of cast-on stitches, plus 1 extra stitch (the original slip knot does not count as a stitch). Cut the scrap yarn, leaving a 6-inch (15 cm) tail.

On the next row, drop the slip knot and gently pull it out.

BACKWARD LOOP METHOD

1. Wrap the working yarn around your thumb clockwise.

2. Insert the right needle into the loop purl-wise. Slide the loop onto the needle.

Repeat steps 1 and 2 until you have the desired number of stitches.

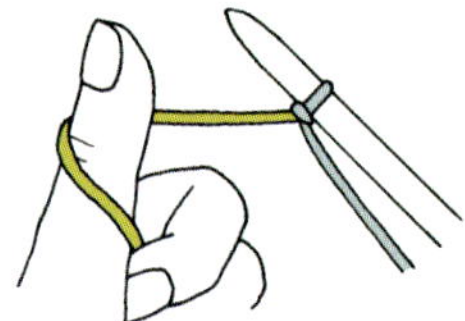

CABLE METHOD

1. Insert the right needle in between the first and second stitch on the left needle.

2. Loosely wrap the working yarn around the needle and pull the stitch through onto the right needle. One stitch cast on.

3. Slip stitch from the right needle to the left needle. Cable cast ons tend to be tight, so make sure to leave a little room between the stitches on the needle. In other words, don't snug them together too closely.

Repeat steps 1–3 until you have the desired number of stitches.

KNITTED CAST ON

1. Insert the right needle into the first stitch on the left needle.

2. Wrap the working yarn around the needle as you would to knit and pull the stitch through onto the right needle.

3. Slip stitch from the right needle to the left needle. One stitch cast on.

Repeat steps 1–3 until you have the desired number of stitches.

Bind Offs

JENY'S SURPRISINGLY STRETCHY BIND OFF

KNIT STITCH

1. Knit 1 stitch.
2. Yarnover backward by beginning with the yarn in the back of your work and wrapping it over and under the needle.

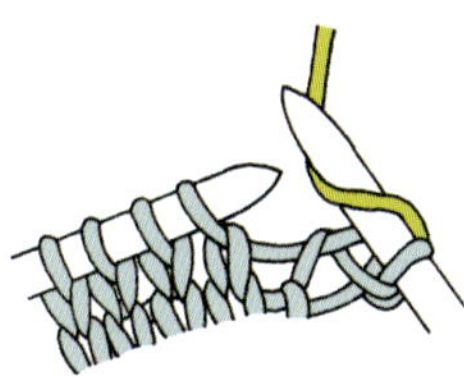

3. Knit 1 stitch. Insert the left needle into the backward yarnover and into the first stitch on the right needle. Pass the backward yarnover and the first stitch over; 1 stitch is bound off.

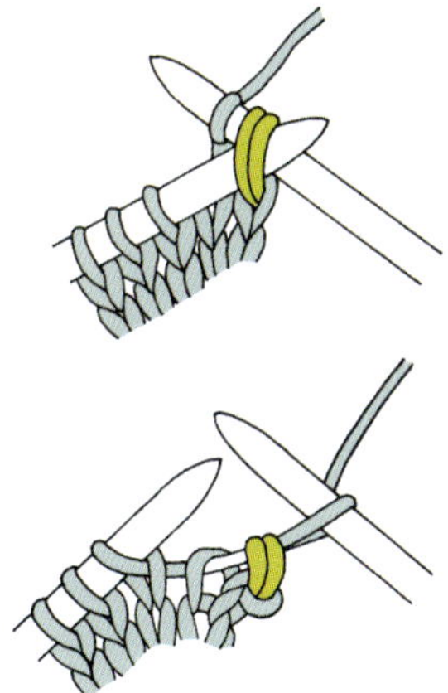

PURL STITCH

1. Purl 1 stitch.
2. Yarnover, bringing the yarn up and over the right needle, from front to back.

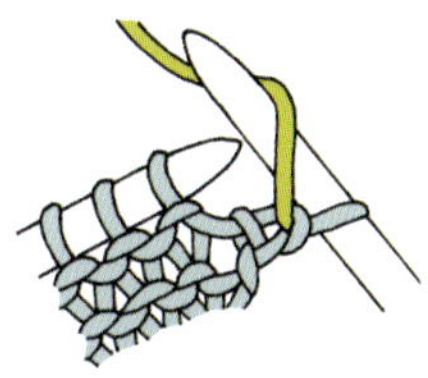

3. Purl 1 stitch. Insert the left needle into the yarnover and the first stitch on the right needle. Pass the yarnover and the first stitch over the last purl stitch; 1 stitch is bound off.

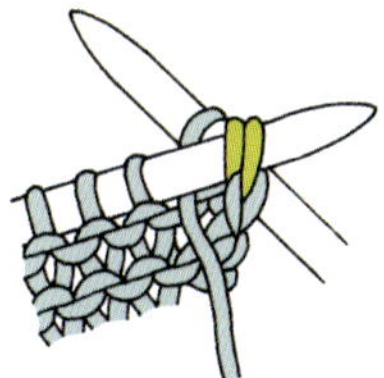

FOR BOTH KNIT AND PURL STITCHES

Repeat steps 2 and 3 until all stitches are bound off. Cut the working yarn, leaving a 12-inch (30 cm) tail, and pull it through the live stitch.

PICOT BIND OFF

This bind off is worked on a multiple of 3 stitches.

1. Using the Knitted method (see "Knitted Cast On"), cast on 2 stitches to the left needle.
2. Bind off 5 stitches (see "Regular Bind Off"). Slip last bound-off stitch back to left needle.

Repeat steps 1 and 2 until all stitches are bound off. Cut the working yarn, leaving a 12-inch (30 cm) tail, and pull it through the live stitch.

REGULAR BIND OFF

K1, *K1, pass first stitch over the second; repeat from * until all stitches are bound off. Cut the working yarn, leaving a 12-inch (30 cm) tail, and pull it through the live stitch.

NEATENING BIND OFF IN THE ROUND

1. After completing the bind off and before weaving in the end, thread the tail from the bind off through a tapestry needle.
2. Slip the tapestry needle from front to back under both legs of the first bound-off stitch and pull the yarn all the way through.
3. Slip the tapestry needle through the center of the last bound-off stitch. Pull the working yarn all the way through to create a new stitch, being sure that it is the same size as the other bound-off stitches. Weave in the end.

Circular Knitting

STOCKINETTE STITCH IN THE ROUND

To work stockinette in the round, knit every stitch in every round for the desired length.

GARTER STITCH IN THE ROUND

To work garter stitch in the round, work the following two-round repeat:

Round 1: Knit to end of round.

Round 2: Purl to end of round.

Repeat Rounds 1 & 2 for the desired length.

If you are beginning or continuing garter stitch after joining a cowlette in the round, begin with a purl round.

Shaping Increases

KNIT-FRONT-AND-BACK (KFB)

Knit into the stitch as usual and leave it on the left needle. With the right needle, knit into the back loop of the same stitch, then slip it off the needle. (1 stitch increased to 2 stitches)

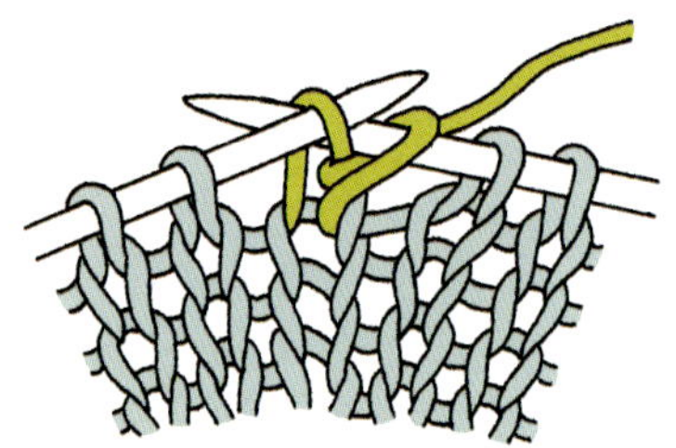

KNIT-FRONT-SLIP-BACK (KFSB)

Knit into the stitch as usual and leave it on the left needle. Insert the right needle into the back loop of the same stitch, then slip it off the needle. (1 stitch increased to 2 stitches)

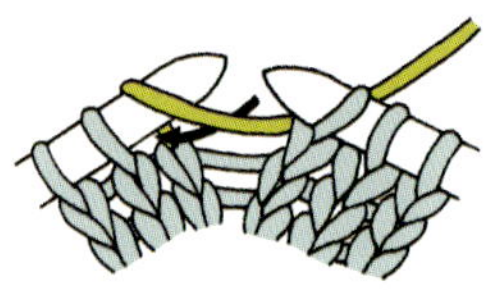

MAKE 1 RIGHT (M1R)

1. Insert the left needle into the strand of yarn between the next two stitches, from back to front.

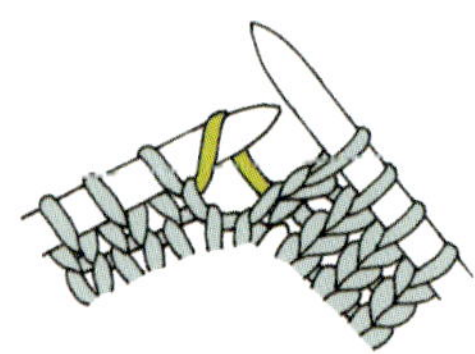

2. Knit into the front leg of this strand. This makes an increase that leans to the right. (1 stitch increased)

MAKE 1 LEFT (M1L)

1. Insert the left needle into the strand of yarn between the next two stitches, from front to back.

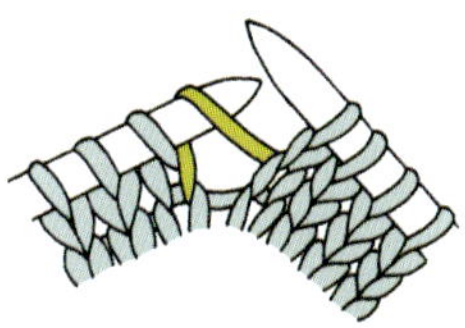

2. Knit into the back leg of this strand. This makes an increase that leans to the left. (1 stitch increased)

YARNOVER (YO)

Bring the yarn to the front of the work between the tip of the needles; let it drape over the needle to the back as you work the next stitch. (1 stitch increased)

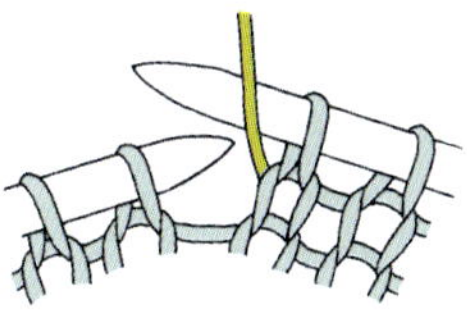

YARNOVER TWICE (YO TWICE)

Bring the yarn to the front of the work between the tip of the needles and wrap it over the right needle from front to back. Repeat this motion, creating two loops, and allow the yarn to drape over the needle to the back as you work the next stitch. (2 stitches increased)

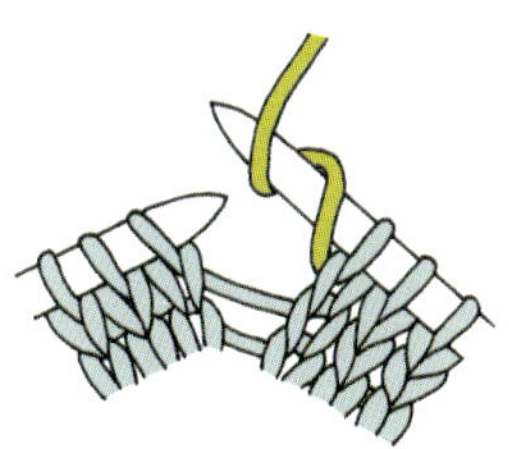

Decreases

KNIT 2 TOGETHER (K2TOG)

Insert the right needle knitwise into the first two stitches on the left needle. Knit the two stitches together. This makes a decrease that leans to the right on the right side of the fabric. (1 stitch decreased)

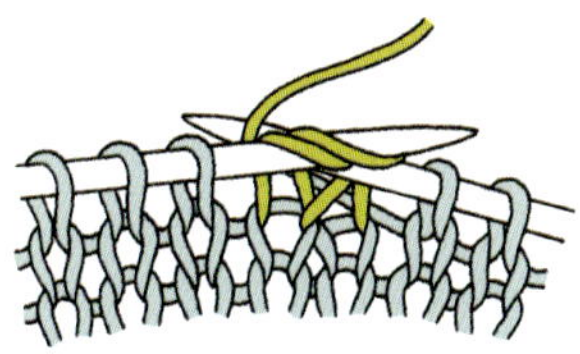

PURL 2 TOGETHER (P2TOG)

Insert the right needle purlwise into the first two stitches on the left needle. Purl them together. When worked on the wrong side of the fabric, this makes a decrease that leans to the right on the right side of the fabric. (1 stitch decreased)

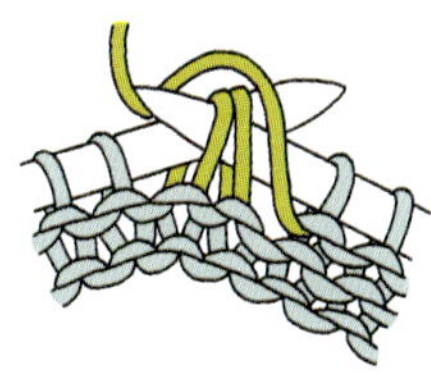

SLIP, SLIP, KNIT (SSK)

Slip the first stitch knitwise, slip the second stitch knitwise; return both stitches to the left needle without twisting them and knit both together through the back loop. This makes a decrease that leans to the left on the right side of the fabric. (1 stitch decreased)

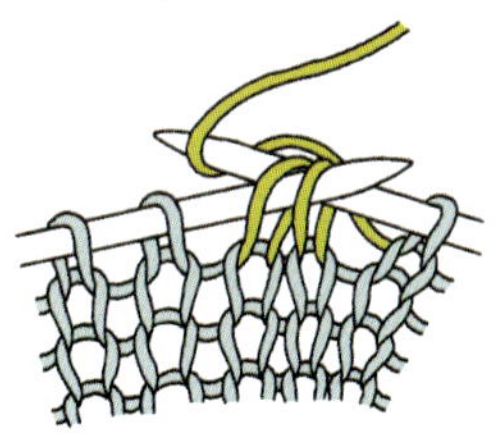

SLIP 2, KNIT 1, PASS 2 SLIPPED STITCHES OVER (S2KP2)

Slip the first two stitches knitwise, knit the next stitch, and pass the two slipped stitches over and off the needle (as you would when binding off). This makes a double decrease. (2 stitches decreased)

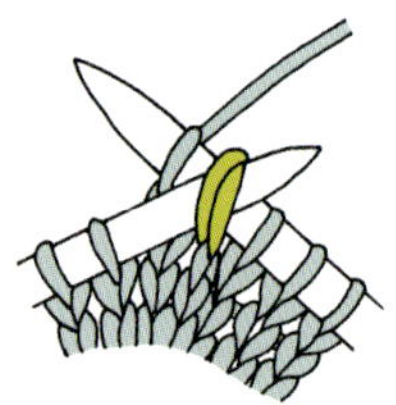

Seams

MATTRESS STITCH

1. With right sides facing up, lay the two pieces side by side on a flat surface.
2. Starting at the bottom of the pieces, insert a threaded tapestry needle under the horizontal strand running between the first and second column of stitches on the left piece. Pull the yarn all the way through, leaving a 6-inch (15 cm) tail.
3. Bring the tapestry needle through the horizontal strand between the first and second column of stitches on the right piece.
4. Continue in this manner, sewing under just one strand on each side with every stitch until you reach the top of the seam, leaving a 6-inch (15 cm) tail.
5. Weave the beginning and ending tails into the wrong side of your knitting.

Other Techniques

PICK UP AND KNIT

Insert your needle through an edge stitch. Wrap the yarn around the needle and knit the stitch on the right side of the fabric. Repeat until you have the desired number of stitches.

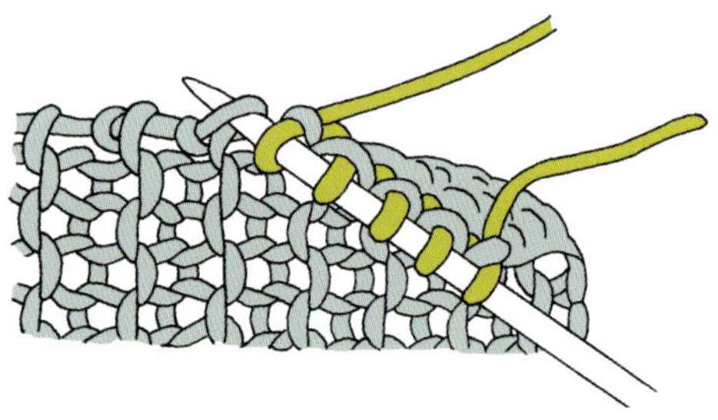

CABLE 6 BACK (C6B) AND CABLE 6 FRONT (C6F)

1. Slip 3 stitches onto a cable needle. Hold the cable needle at the back of your work (for a C6B) or at the front of your work (for a C6F).
2. Knit the next three stitches off the left needle.
3. Knit the 3 stitches off the cable needle.

ELONGATED STITCH (KW2)

1. Insert right needle into the stitch as if to knit.
2. Wrap the working yarn twice around the right needle before pulling the stitch through. There should now be two loops on the right needle.
3. On the next row/round, knit into the first loop and drop the extra loop, creating one long stitch.

WEAVING IN ENDS

In stockinette and garter (A), choose a row of purl bumps on the wrong side of the fabric and use a tapestry needle to weave the tail under and over each purl bump. In ribbing (B), choose a column of knit stitches on the wrong side of the fabric, near the tail. Use a tapestry needle to weave the tail in and out of each knit stitch in the column.

A

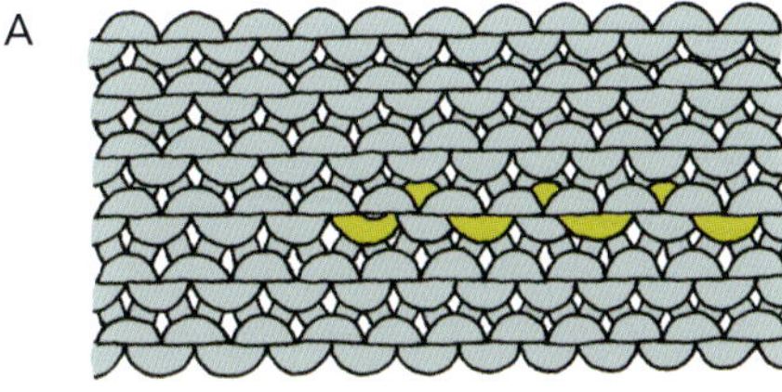

B

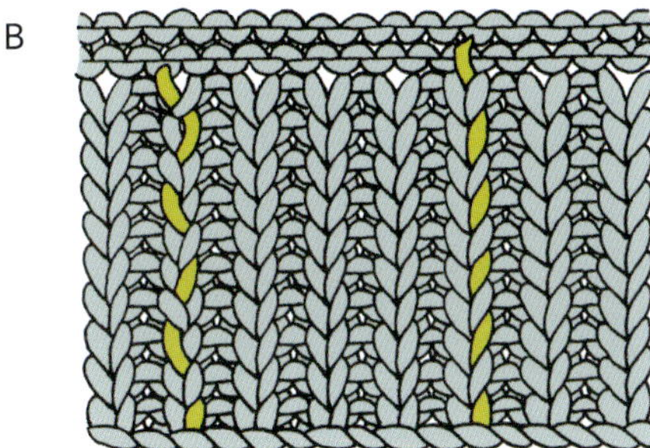

Abbreviations

BOR Beginning of round

C6B Cable 6 back

C6F Cable 6 front

k Knit

kw2 Elongated stitch

k2tog Knit 2 stitches together (1 stitch decreased)

kfb Knit into front and back of the same stitch (1 stitch increased)

kfsb Knit into front and slip the back of same stitch (1 stitch increased)

m Marker

m1 Make 1 stitch in the direction of your choice (1 stitch increased); keep increase direction consistent within pattern

m1l Make 1 left (1 stitch increased)

m1r Make 1 right (1 stitch increased)

mb Make bobble

p Purl

p2tog Purl 2 stitches together (1 stitch decreased)

pm Place marker

RS Right side

s2kp2 Slip 2 stitches, knit 1, pass 2 slipped stitches over (2 stitches decreased)

sl Slip 1 stitch purlwise, unless otherwise stated

sm Slip marker

ssk Slip 2 stitches knitwise 1 at a time, knit both stitches together through the back loop (1 stitch decreased)

st(s) Stitch(es)

tbl Through back loop(s)

WS Wrong side

wyib With yarn in back

wyif With yarn in front

yo Yarnover

Cowlette Patterns by Shape

Triangle (Kerchief)

Triangle (Poncho)

Half-Pi

Heart

Featured Yarns and Supplies

All of the cowlettes in this book were knit using yarn provided by the generous companies below.

Blue Sky Fibers
blueskyfibers.com

Katia Yarns
katia.com

Kelbourne Woolens
kelbournewoolens.com

Madelinetosh
madelinetosh.com

Manos del Uruguay
manos.uy

Neighborhood Fiber Co.
neighborhoodfiberco.com

Quince & Co.
quinceandco.com

Rowan
knitrowan.com

Thank you to Addi for providing the knitting needles, Cocoknits for the notions, and Katrinkles for the buttons.

Addi
addi.de/en

Cocoknits
cocoknits.com

Katrinkles
katrinkles.com

Acknowledgments

I would like to thank my very attentive and talented editor, Emily Spiegelman, who always seems to think of everything, and my art director, Bredna Lago, for her acute attention to detail. And thank you to my eagle-eyed tech editors Kristina McGrath and Sarah Walworth for ensuring pattern accuracy. And of course, thanks to the rest of the staff at Storey Publishing for their hard work and endless kindness.

I would like to thank my husband, Jake, for letting me borrow his neck to test cowlette sizes at all hours of the day (and night), and my son, Beau, for cheering me on through my cowlette journey.

Safiyyah Talley

INDEX

Page numbers in italics indicate photos; numbers *in* **bold** indicate charts.

T

U